ADAM RETURNS

&

The Five New Commandments

(The Uniting Testament)

Michael J. Simmons
Channelling Adam

Metaphysical / Self-Help

Copyright © 2025 By Michael J. Simmons
All Rights Reserved.

All rights reserved. No part of this publication may be reproduced, distributed, or transmitted in any form or by any means, including photocopying, recording, or other electronic or mechanical methods, without the prior written permission of the publisher, except in the case of brief quotations embodied in critical reviews and certain other non-commercial uses permitted by copyright law. For permission requests, email the publisher Attention: Permissions requested via the contact page http://www.LivingEternity.com

ISBN: 978-1-7638113-0-0 (Hardcover)

ISBN: 978-1-7638113-2-4 (Paperback)

ISBN: 978-1-7638113-6-2 (E-book)

Book design by Michael J Simmons

Gold Coast, Queensland, Australia.

Int Phone: (+61) 401 356 323

www.LivingEternity.com

Dedication

Thanks God

About the Author

The Spirit of Adam is the Spirit in me, and together we're here to replant the seed! It's the seed of no greed from the fruit from the tree in the Garden.

Universal time is again back in sight, and the first man on earth has returned in Spirit. Approved for his intimate knowledge of the garden, Adam returns of his own free will with a quest that has been sanctioned with heavens' blessing.

Adam has returned to inspire mankind and to reignite the flame of life. His charge is to reinstall hope and faith, and his mission is to guide mankind back from the brink of extinction.

Adam brings with him Five New Commandments and his arrival is to serve as a reminder that the heavens are present and closely monitoring our celestial home. The Orb Eden!

Hold on tight as your halo starts to shine. Be drawn back into the light and walk as one with the Spirit of Adam, together back into Eternity.

Whilst this reopens our world to divine intervention, independent free will is still very much in play; all souls wanting, every soul willing, and any souls asking will have an equal opportunity to find their way back into the present, the now and indeed this moment to awaken back into their being.

Wide awake and conscious of karmic choices, conscious of their capacity to give and to receive, looking to assist and facilitate change where their skills are needed, and their karmic value known. It is here that those hearts will find home.

- By will they will come, and by will they will go. This is the gift of the heavens on show.

- Karma is known as the soul's right to claim; doing what matters will see the soul gain.

- Adam returns with a very heavy heart; Eden is spent and needs to restart.

Adam expects some beings will willingly remain in the shadows, and others will willingly fall on their swords. It is known that some will choose to ignore, ignorance and arrogance scored as a flaw.

With our world consumed with greed, corruption, and chaos, humanity now has one last fighting chance to extend our otherwise doomed existence. A conscious and concerted effort is required to repair with care our lands to share, to clean our oceans and our seas, to replant the trees to breathe with ease and to honour the flowers with visiting bees.

And now to me, you see, I'm free to be and to receive and Adam requires beings like me. My name is Michael.

I'm conscious of karma and conscious of time. I'm happily married to my beautiful wife, and just like all couples, we've endured some strife. Together, we've helped guide more children than our four, with an amazing extended family that walks through our open doors. Our love is unconditional, but our hearts are often torn.

That's enough about now; let's look at my past. In academics, I was challenged, and in sports was often last. Going back further to where my story begins, I was schooled as a Catholic with the bible bashed in by men in white robes that hid sin within.

Back a little further to when I lost my faith. I was blissfully living, aged seven or eight; when my parents went their separate ways, I was shitty with God and poked my tongue up to space.

I can tell you from then that things only got worse; on the outside, they said normal, but deep inside, I cried, 'I'm cursed', and that's the very moment I first heard my soul in verse.

Then visions started coming. I sensed the devil wanting me; he sought my soul surrendered. Instead, he got my kicks and screams. It willed me wide awake whilst sleeping, and now I'm the Master of my dreams.

Getting back in touch with heaven was the path I chose to take. I freely willed my will away; to God, I begged for Heaven's sake. I'm sorry that I hurt you; I feel I've paid for my mistakes. Forgive yourself. God showed me; he said I'll need this at the gates.

It was then I picked a pen up, and on safari, I explored; in South Africa, I felt it, and on to Egypt, I felt sure. It was way below the desert where I found the unlocked door, with the only friend I had back then, my pen became my sword! At that moment, I awakened; give it to me! God heard my roar. I resurfaced from the sands of time, and my Eternal was restored, with the Holy Spirit present and Adam's spirit now onboard, our rhymes a trail of breadcrumbs on the path back to the Lord.

Table of Contents

Once Upon a Time 1
Authors Message 2
    The Five New Commandments 3
Forward – A Letter to Eve 4
CHAPTER 1: FAITH 7
    A Humane Approach 8
    And then There was Light 9
    Ask for Help 10
    Ask Heaven 11
    As Above so Below 12
    Balanced 13
    Back to The Garden 14
    Blessed 15
    Beyond the Church 16
    Closing Bibles 17
    Commandments 18
    Caution 19
    Compassion 20
    Conviction of the Heart 21
    Cultivating Courage 22
    Divine Disclosure 23
    Divinely Inspired (i) 24
    Divinely Inspired (ii) 25
    Dare to Care 26

Eden in Orbit 27
Enlightened 28
Epiphany 29
Faith 30
Faith Refound 31
Forgive (i) 32
Forgive (ii) 33
Forgiving You (i) 34
Forgiving You (ii) 35
Father 36
Gatekeeper 37
Good Friday 38
Grateful 39
Gratitude 40
Goddess 41
Hallelujah 42
Hearing Heaven 43
Heaven on Eden 44
Holy Spirit 45
I Have a Gift to Share 46
If We Awaken 47
Inner Whispers 48
Inspired 49
It's Time to Pray 50
Judgement Day 51
Leap of Faith 52

Learn to know Spirit	53
Letters from Heaven	54
Light the Path	55
Living in the Son	56
Mantra	57
Mass Consciousness	58
Merry Christmas	59
Mystical Poetry	60
Mysticism	61
Never Alone	62
No Fear	63
Nothing but Love	64
Oh My God	65
Oh when the Saints	66
One Voice	67
Oneness	68
Open Prayer	69
Parable For Peace	70
Peace Perceived	71
Patience	72
Prophetic and Profound	73
Religion	74
Rest in Peace	75
Resurrection	76
Sacrifice	77
Salvation	78

Spirit 79
Spirit Fills the Void 80
Spirit Level 81
Spiritual Growth 82
See beyond the Shadow 83
Stand Firm (i) 84
Stand Firm (ii) 85
Tap into Soul 86
The Antidote 87
The Sacrifice 88
Threading the Camel 89
Transcending Life 90
Transformation 91
Transmit the Truth 92
Unconditional Love 93
Unreservedly Eternal 94
Vibrations 95
Wake Up 96
What would God Do 97
Will you Stand Beside Me 98
Wing and a Prayer 99
Wisdom 100
Witnessing You 101
Yes or No 102

CHAPTER 2: GREED 103
    Alternative World 104
    Attraction 105
    Bet your Bottom Dollar 106
    Bottom Dollar 107
    Boundaries 108
    Celebrity 109
    Consumption 110
    Corrosive 111
    Constant Narrative 112
    Devil in the Details 113
    Desensitised 114
    Detachment 115
    Ego 116
    Eliminate the Ego 117
    Fancy Dress 118
    Fear 119
    Feeling Naked 120
    Fertility 121
    Fragile 122
    Global Warming 123
    Greed 124
    Guilt 125
    Haters 126
    Hierarchy 127

High Society	128
Highly Strung	129
Hunger	130
I Kill Egos	131
Ignorance	132
Indifference	133
Institutes	134
It's all Your Fault	135
Lifting the Curse	136
Lost Soul	137
Malnutrition	138
Mankind Before Money	139
Military	140
No Guarantee	141
No Rhyme or Reason	142
Normality	143
Option One	144
Out of Touch	145
Over One Hundred	146
Pay Attention	147
Population	148
Poverty	149
Power (i)	150
Power (ii)	151
Resources	152
Respect what's Real	153

Sapiens 154

Save the World 155

Seven Deadly 156

Shame on You 157

Societies 158

Subscribe 159

Technology 160

The Powers that Be 161

Tick Tock 162

Tolerance 163

Ultimatum 164

Water 165

Weekend 166

With or Without You 167

CHAPTER 3: PURPOSE **169**
    Adaption 170
    Articulating Being 171
    Artistic 172
    Awareness 173
    Band Together 174
    Be 175
    Be Thankful 176
    Be your Best Self 177
    Bridge of Knowledge 178
    Build the Stairs 179
    Calibrate your Way 180
    Care 181
    Challenge Reality 182
    Challenge Yourself 183
    Change the World 184
    Channeling 185
    Character Revealed 186
    Conceptualise 187
    Conditioned 188
    Conducting Life 189
    Competency 190
    Cultivate 191
    Direction of Life 192
    Disclosure 193

Discovery 194

Distribute 195

Driving Lessons...196

Empower Others...197

Energy 198

Existence 199

Experience 200

Focused 201

Free Will..202

Freedom...203

Fill in the Future...204

Find your Purpose 205

Footprints 206

Foresight..207

Frequency 208

Genuine 209

Go the Distance 210

Going Forward 211

Greater Space 212

Here and Now..213

Highest Order 214

House in Order 215

Human Being 216

Human Capacity..217

I am Speaking to You 218

I'm Here to Change the World.................................219

Identification	220
Intention	221
Intentions	222
It Takes its Toll	223
Keep it Simple	224
Leading Edge	225
Lessons and Blessings	226
Let Me In	227
Let's Get Creative	228
Life	229
Look at your Life	230
Manifested for You	231
Moral Courage	232
Mother	233
Moving Forward	234
My Free Will	235
Navigation	236
New Dawn	237
No Regrets	238
Not A Soul	239
Optimisation	240
Our Home	241
Painting with Words	242
Parenting	243
Permission Granted	244
Personalities	245

Philosophically Present	246
Pitch it to the People	247
Potent Potential	248
Present (i)	249
Present (ii)	250
Present (iii)	251
Present the Present	252
Redesign	253
Refined Being	254
Relight your Flame	255
Remain Conscious	256
Rhythm of Life	257
Say Thank You (i)	258
Say Thank You (ii)	259
Screaming Soul	260
Shadow Known	261
Shadow Work	262
Soul Science	263
Soulful Sensation	264
Soulfully Being	265
Small Steps	266
Stand Alone	267
Sensitive	268
Take a Breath	269
The Big Picture	270
The First Words	271

The Gift of Giving 272
Therapy 273
This is My Art 274
This life is about You 275
Trailblazing 276
Tune In 277
Turnaround 278
Turn toward Being 279
Unite 280
What I Do 281
What is Art 282
What really Matters 283
Who Are You 284
Windows In 285
Words I've Written 286

CHAPTER 4: HOPE 287
    Abundance 288
    All Aboard 289
    All We Need is Hope 290
    Beautifully Broken 291
    Beautiful Soul 292
    Behind the Gates 293
    Behind the Mask 294
    Being Human 295
    Believe It or Not 296
    Breaking Hearts 297
    Broken Soul 298
    Celebrate Today 299
    Children 300
    Coincidence 301
    Colour Blind 302
    Connected 303
    Conscience 304
    Consistency 305
    Contemplate 306
    Cosmos 307
    Countdown 308
    Created Evolution 309
    Cycle has Closed 310
    Darkness 311

Darkness Dawns 312

Dream 313

Deeply Connected 314

Down the Rabbit Hole 315

Dust to Dust 316

Death 317

Emotion 318

Emotions 319

Empathy Rising 320

Empty Chair 321

Encouraged 322

Epilogue 323

Euphoria 324

Evolution 325

Exit Time 326

Fearless 327

Feeling for Real 328

Find Me 329

Find the Beauty 330

Find the Positive 331

Fire 332

Full Emotions 333

Go with the Flow 334

Goodwill Matters 335

Google Homepage 336

Grounded 337

Happily Ever After 338
Heart Attack 339
History 340
Homeward Bound 341
Honesty 342
Human Spirit 343
Humanism 344
Humanity 345
Image 346
In Times of Doubt 347
Instinct 348
It's not Rocket Science 349
It's Time 350
Lifetime 351
Listen Intently 352
Living Eternity 353
Moments 354
Nothingness 355
Now 356
Nursery Rhyme 357
Osmosis 358
Out of this World 359
Over the Rainbow 360
Premonition 361
Remember to Imagine 362
Rise and Shine 363

Roller Coaster	364
Shine and Guide	365
Shoot for a Star	366
Soul in Flight	367
Soul Lost	368
Suffer Less	369
Symphony	370
Surrender	371
Synchronicity	372
There's a Finish Line	373
This is Eden	374
This is how you do It	375
Together	376
Unbelievable	377
Victory	378
Wipe the Sleep Away	379
Wonder (i)	380
Wonder (ii)	381
Willing and Able	382
You are Dying	383

Once Upon a Time

Open your mind to this story
Narrated by your soul
Consciousness approaching
Entertain a common goal

Universal times upon us
Prepare to be and be amazed
Oneness offers new horizons
Navigation through the maze

Absolute in your conviction

Tenacious in your stance
Intent to beat indifference
Mediocre stands no chance
End this story to advance

Authors Message

I welcome your soul be it sinner through saint
I welcome the meek and the mild and greats
I welcome the wealthy to share if you choose
I welcome all nations to cease your disputes
I welcome the aged to display right to youth
I welcome those broken or lost and confused
I welcome the outlaws and those that police
I welcome the parents with kids wanting peace
I welcome all Muslims and Christians and Jews
I welcome the Buddhists to pray with Hindus
I welcome the sane and insane and restrained
I welcome mind doctors to doctors of brains
I welcome the sceptics who seek to believe
I welcome the dying to leave here at ease
I welcome churchgoers and practicing priests
I welcome the carers and those thought of least
I welcome the drunk and drug takers with care
I welcome the triers who try in despair
I welcome the poet's and artisan scribe's
I welcome the dreamers and artists who strive
I welcome peacemakers who've put up a fight
I welcome the darkest of souls who can't hide
I welcome the wanderers back who have roamed
I welcome you walk with me lovingly home

The Five New Commandments

11th Commandment is faith
Faith is needed to succeed

12th Commandment is fixed
Do not follow in mans greed

13th Commandment is for you to explore
Stay within boundaries or fall on your sword

14th Commandment is protection from treason
Seek only your purpose and not for lives reason

15th Commandment is the last for survival
Be in sync with your soul before judged on arrival

Forward – A Letter to Eve

Dearest Eve,

I shall cherish the honour to scribe in this book, with the strength of an army, your consent overlooked. As I draw up the oceans the salt will remain. A cryptic saline solution floats all to the mermaid's dismay.

Do not be disenchanted, I am extending my hand, for I have been to the mountains and explored all of land, and I have done it but thrice to help you understand.

I use Grand Master illusion to execute each escape, first your prince under your wing, but never your king you did state. But as King I kept record of your songs teaching false fate, your songs lead the weak, the weak souls you take.

Way back then again when you offered the mask for my task, as man I dove in, and the insight was vast, as you answer with truth all the questions I asked.

Be it then again when, next time or today, four words we did share 'for protection we'll stay,' in this parallel time we first flew separate ways.

To the second by choice, we did land in the garden. You could hear the snake's voice causing your soul to harden. A dilemma! Use my faith and in God seek your pardon but you stood behind snake, cryptic fear I did see as you willed snake to guard forbidden fruit in the tree, I've no fear of snake! It is your greed that intrigued. Knowing up until then we shared all that we need.

From then I did pace, as I questioned your haste till the instant I stopped, watching rotten fruit drop. Like a bomb it did hit me, the fruits overripe, fruit not suited for picking but the seed inside is all right! The seed of no greed, kept from you out of sight. Breaking down all that happened, I again gained free insight!

You did not need me here anymore and so I wandered off alone. Doomed with no chance for forgiveness, thrice I lived and died alone. Life to bone! Life to bone! Life to bone!

The third time we met, a new moon reached its crest, and I took the form wild dog! I did why For I heard your howl as I learned to growl, and to the moon you would cry for insight. It was then you gave freely insight to see clearly, the cycle of the moon.

With only one month to succeed in this hunt, from that moment I started to groom. I followed your pack, used my sense to stay back, and in the darkness I did loom. For my knowledge was guaranteed doom.

So, I used the next month to succeed in my hunt and I frolicked for fun in your scent. Satisfied your pack was not wise, with the moon due to rise, I present. We crossbred as wild wolves in disguise.

It is blue blood I did pledge as I leapt off the edge, to your amazement your eyes watched me fly. I have again flown a long way, landing safely to say, you can again regain faith as insight.

Adam

CHAPTER 1:
FAITH

A Humane Approach

A dedication to humanity

Humbled truly by this gift
Used strict for good intention
Mankind is lost and needs a lift
Awake and then awaken
No soul missing from the list
Every soul deserves their halo

A newfound reason to exist
Pray with love and good intention
Practice patience as we shift
Rest in times of doubt
Organise your route
Assist all others as we drift
Coexistence is the answer
Heaven sends this gift if wished

And then There was Light

Alive to awaken the sleepers
Neighbours and family and friends
Deliver yourself from lives bondage

Think of mankind on the mend
Heavens applauding your courage
Eternals the path to present
Neglecting this is at your peril

Too late for some souls to transcend
Hear what I'm saying is gospel
End this flight in the light at the end
Rest in peace and not begging for pardon
Eternal you'll fly once again

Will again that you're willing and ready
Ask heaven that Angels be sent
Show up and shine bright with your halo

Light the path for mankind to repent
Ignite and relight other spirits
Giveaway the free halos till spent
Honour Father as heaven and Mother as earth
Take a bow and bow out to ascend

Ask for Help

Advance by gifting more than given
Spirit by your side and strong
Keep your faith fixed and stay focused

Fame and fortune thoughts are wrong
Only ask for what is needed
Receive with thanks well in advance

Heavy is the cross you carry
Exceeding greed is the command
Light the pathway back to heaven
Pray for the day they lend a hand

Ask Heaven

Answers sure and ready
Simply ask to know your soul
Kneeling shows commitment

Hallelujah you control
Elevate your spirit
Ask at night and throughout the day
Value heavens answers
Every answer lights the way
Navigate your way to stay

As Above so Below

At the core you're enlightened
Seated here is your soul

An abundance of wisdom
Bounty far beyond gold
Orientate your own way in
Values held in turn hold
Exponential these values

Senseless value if cold
One thing to remember

Balance back to behold
Eternal endurance
Live and let life evolve
One thing to forget is
Worth can be bought and can be sold

Balanced

Begin with no judgement
Allow all to be
Live and let live
Adaptation is key
Need only what's needed
Concede if it's greed
Endearing to others
Disposition to bequeath

Back to The Garden

Back to basics
All in and Godspeed
Consoling each soul
Keep safe and proceed

Together the goal
Oasis from greed

The old story solved
He's alive and flies free
Expressive when told

God's gift indeed
Archaic this wisdom
Replanting the seed
Directed by Heaven
Eden allows us to breathe
Nature best nurtures with need

Blessed

Bestowed empathetic
Loving all life on board
Eternal life living
Success assured
Souls seeking salvation
Expect a reward
Divine life you'll live by accord

Beyond the Church

Be a beacon for those seeking
Eight billion bodies bound for bone
Your birth on Earth's for lessons
On one's own but not alone
No greater gift than God's good grace
Divine design defines this zone

Trek back on track to heaven
Harvest all the love you've sown
Every moment here's eternal

Christ himself a cornerstone
Honor being and believing
Use your time here to atone
Reach out for spark with spirit
Collect good karma as you roam
Help the lost and sick and lonely make it home

Closing Bibles

Captured for reference
Lamenting old ways
Organised violence
Sin on display
Its long lost its meaning
Not needed today
God is within

Bibles now in decay
Instrumental it has been
Best in its day
Let go and begin
Exist and create
Subscribe now to faith

Commandments

Code of conduct for humanity
Our free will will will away
Motivation for all mankind
Moral compass lights the way
Absolution comes with progress
Navigation your mainstay
Direct your own eternal
Manifesting day to day
Each and every precious moment
Now your presents on display
Temptations hone your lessons
Score awarding thanks and praise

Caution

Consider this a warning
Action call to those awake
Understand this is your calling
Think inside which choice to make
I for one am standing
One and all needs to partake
Needed now for goodness's sake

Compassion

Consequential recognition
Observing karmic flaws
Manifest corrective lessons
Painful moments seek the core
Absolution for transgressions
Sins need a pardon or remorse
Suffering goes hand in hand
I am that I am the law
Observers see the way home
Navigators show the shore

Conviction of the Heart

Comprehension here is needed
Open hearts will open doors
Needs we need be met by many
Versus greedy overlords
Intentions meant to be disruptive
Calling out from deep within
Talk the truth and speak with reason
If deemed greedy then it's sin
Offer strategies and guidance
Name the ones you think should share

Observe those hiding in the shadows
Forgo the ones you know don't care

Time to turn as one together
Humankind commands repair
Every one of us here suffers

Hearts all bleeding in despair
End this pain with strong conviction
Action call to all awake
Rise as one to help the healing
The time is now for goodness's sake

Cultivating Courage

Contagious compassion
Unrelenting desire
Leaving breadcrumbs for others
Talking truths that inspire
Instructions for mankind
Validating true wealth
Aligning with spirit
Think the world back to health
Information for seekers
Nothing left than to choose
Gift the world your best effort

Courageous souls never lose
Open gates into heaven
Unite sees you strive
Righteous revival
Atonement alive
Gallantry living
Enter inside

Divine Disclosure

Directions straight from heaven
Instructions for mankind to use
Vindicate yourself whilst living
Insist on ceasing self-abuse
Nothing worthy will come easy
Empathise with those in pain

Do what's right in every instance
Insightful soul within to claim
Spirit always there for guidance
Close your eyes and pray to wake
Let your love be overflowing
One day you'll need this at the gates
Send daily praise to heaven
Understand this shows you're true
Receive more blessings when you're giving
Enlightened being your choice to choose

Divinely Inspired (i)

Devoted to a better world
Implicating greed
Visions seen preceding Eden
Intelligence cannot see
Nor can walking sleepers
Eternal only seen a dream
Lucid moments rouse a waking soul
Youth deceived and put to sleep

Insight comes as you awaken
No longer sleeping easily
Seeing suffering and sorrow
Painful is reality
Inspired and enlightened
Reverence to heaven is the key
Eternal is the woken soul
Defined divinity

Divinely Inspired (ii)

Deep and meaningful mystic
Insightful and sincere
Visualisations of a better life
Informing as a seer
Nothing other than enlightening
Expressing to cohere
Live in love and offer guidance
Youth be shown to persevere

Invest and live aligned with elders
Nurture both to tune-in clear
Spirit strong and reconnected
Practice prayers and praise whilst here
Incorporating oneness
Respectful of the sphere
Entertaining no indifference
Denouncing life of fear

Dare to Care

Dip your toe into the deep end
Alarmed by feelings of despair
Rekindle hope and faith with kindness
End this hopeless lack of care

Think of those in need of healing
Overflows your heart to share

Caress your soul so ever gently
A sense of urgency is there
Rest assured by being present
Empathic soul repaired

Eden in Orbit

Existence is endangered
Driven by man to the brink
Empty souls with greedy goals
No time to stop and think

Insidious is their nature
Nature suffers their disease

Orbit soon for them aborted
Relief for Eden's trees and bees
Back to basics for the chosen
Indifference they'll have healed
Thanking God to whom they yield

Enlightened

Expect to find the mystic
Nestle in to find your soul
Love must be unconditional
Inner wisdom is the goal
God is here and waiting for you
Heaven's stairs are here to build
Think of this as inner work
Engineer you're being skilled
Nothing needed than commitment
Eternal knowledge here fulfilled
Direct yourself here with free will

Epiphany

Existentialism for reference
Philosophical approach
Infinite awareness
Prestigious amongst most
Heaven sent for coaching
Amazing is this grace
No need for confirmation
Yesteryears of sin erased

Faith

Fantastical fact
Archaic indeed
I am that I am
That I am that you need
Holy are thee

Faith Refound

Forevermore here grateful
Affirmed to living life with love
Indifference long forgotten
Taking strides within above
Heaven is the destination

Romance the thought of reaching there
End your days here in this knowledge
Faith here fixed shows you're prepared
Onboard Earth is not forever
Universal is your soul
Navigate your life eternal
Done with faith and life is solved

Forgive (i)

Free your being from its bondage
Old pain inside should be let go
Reawake to life eternal
Grief when carried makes you slow
It's important you move freely
Visualise all blame behind
Eternal life here you will find

Forgive (ii)

Find peace within by feeling
Original sin erased
Repetition now repealing
Graced with amazing grace
Intentions govern healing
Vision of the gates
Each in their own escapade

Forgiving You (i)

Faith driven healing
Ordained to forgive
Romance the feeling
Guidelines to live
Insightful revelation
Vested to save
Internal instructions
New pathways to pave
Go forth and prosper

You're free from enslaved
Only you can forgive you
Unparalleled faith

Forgiving You (ii)

Fruit once deemed forbidden
Offered now free to heal
Replanted in Eden
Guilt free and surreal
It's your path to be pardoned
Valued far beyond gold
Inner forgiveness
No strings involved
God's greatest gift of guidance

Your sins all reprieved
Onwards toward heaven
Unless you choose greed

Father

Fight or flight his instinct
Adoration as a sire
Tactical in conflict
Heroic if inspired
Ego present without conscience
Resolute to be desired

Gatekeeper

Guardians of eternal
Armoured gates of time
Trespass not an option
Each soul in leaves dark behind
Karmic each soul's journey
Each to their own to choose inside
Eternity's the reward
Perpetual its design
Entry terms collect your halo
Respect all those in front in line

Good Friday

God showed again his brilliance
Offered us a man who seen
Open to the next dimension
Dimensions are no fantasy

Faith is the only way in
Righteous way installed in dreams
In plain sight is well insight
Dabble in and question me
Awaken to tomorrow
Yes you are allowed to be

Grateful

Gifted with a precious moment
Recognise each moment's new
Appreciate these rare occasions
Take the chance to say thank you
Express your inner warmth and feelings
Find a way to show your praise
Use your soulful raw emotions
Let your soul be on display

Gratitude

Grateful for breathing
Recognition of life
Atonement for the soul
Testament to be nice
Insurmountable vision
Tactful and true
Unequivocal statement
Divine point of view
Expressing thank you

Goddess

Gender has never been the issue
Oneness takes the force of two
Don't ever second-guess her
Delivery done of me and you
Equally eternal
Self-realised and absolute
She is perfectly astute

Hallelujah

Heaven sent me to find you
All aboard will soon see
Love is the answer
Love is the key
Eternal the dance
Let go and let be
Understand stand beside me
Justified to fly free
A perpetual gift
Hold faith tight and believe

Hearing Heaven

Hearts must be open to receiving
Ego must be known or been let go
A prayer petitioned must stay open
Reserve your soul to stay on show
It's through spirit you'll hear heaven
Noble minds can hear with ease
God has given us the channels

Heaven helps if you say please
Each and every soul can listen
Angels calling you will hear
Victory for man they're chanting
End the suffering they cheer
Name your worth to tune-in clear

Heaven on Eden

Humanity needs you
Each and every way
Archetypal being
Visually on display
Empty chair challenge
Needs no throne or pew

Offer a spot for your spirit
Now one becomes two

Express inward or outward
Do what feels right in you
Enlightenment offered
Nothing needed but truth

Holy Spirit

Highest of Angels
Overseer of sin
Linguistic mystic
Your guardian within

Saint maker of soldiers
Promoter of light
Impeccable stature
Righteous done right
Inspector of halos
Top tactician in flight

I Have a Gift to Share

It's not about me

How I think
And what I've thought
Vivid imaging seen
Every dream believed

Awake asleep or in-between

God answered my prayers to be taught
Instinctive perception
From birth to behold
Talking inside of truth

Talking faith to the cold
Of the options within

Simply ask and be told
Happy feelings depend
And emotions unfold
Recognise you and I am
Every adult and child

If We Awaken

It's about thinking like Plato
Feeling like Jesus

Waking the sleepers
Eternally living

A brand-new beginning
Waking the sleepers
All in and all sure
Keep the faith and stand tall
End greed whilst living
No longer sinning

Inner Whispers

Insightful interruptions
Narrating present out aloud
Nobody else can hear it
Expressing things and thoughts profound
Recalibrate your mindset

Wake your soul by being true
Human being being human
It asks that you connect with truth
Survey the walking sleepers
Pressing snooze will see you loose
Eagerly awaken
Raise your Spirit if you do
Spoken truth is within you

Inspired

Indifference the issue
Need to fix this at last
Sweeping changes required
Put the past in the past
It's as simple as starting
Recognise you're the seed
Educate by example
Don't take more than you need

It's Time to Pray

I'll share with you the process
Take a deep breath to tune in
Surrender to your heart space

This is how true prayers begin
Imagine heaven's listening
Mind your thoughts don't drift away
Elevate to your higher self

Think to thank God for each day
On offer is salvation

Praise is something shared each way
Receive the light to be enlightened
Accept that guidance you'll obey...
Yield to God's will when you pray

Judgement Day

Join the queue that best describes you
Use your manners whilst in line
Discuss your way to the turnstile
Gain advancement if inclined
Enter the chamber
Meet and greet those inside
Engage in self-judgement
Next to centre says goodbye
Twelfth soul in may need assurance

Decide amongst you who'll advise
Approach those at the turnstile
You'll need the twelfth in to rise

Leap of Faith

Love lets you see heaven
Eternal your gaze
All be in believing
People have faith

Open your heart
Fathom your fate

Free if believed in
Amazing grace
Infinite options
Take a leap and escape
Halo on on display

Learn to know Spirit

Live to learn in every moment
Expect to see beyond despair
Advance as one toward heaven
Realise that you've spirit there
Nothing needed than your free will

Treat each moment as so rare
Open hearts will find alignment

Keeping faith here shows you care
Navigate with ease with spirit
Oneness takes the form of two
Want for nothing and owe no one

Spirit freely shining through
Present prophetic and profoundly
Insync as one and speaking true
Revelations to reveal
Intentions clear and right on cue
Trust the Spirit you've within that's guiding you

Letters from Heaven

Love all is the message
Every soul in love will heal
Think to thank the heavens
Take a deep breath in to feel
Exhale gently like the trees breathe
Realise your being's part of life
Symbiotic romance

Forgotten love has bought you strife
Resume your lost connection
Oneness comes to you in waves
Mindfulness brings magic

Heavens watching your display
Earn karma whilst you're being
Attractive souls will lead the way
Value every precious moment
Expect that some by choice remain
Now it's time to love again

Light the Path

Let go of fear and worry
Ignite your halo to shine bright
Groundwork is now completed
Heavens steps are now in sight
Tell the world its heaven calling

Tell hearts heavy they need spark
Help the sick and lost and lonely
Empathise with soul's still dark

Practice patience as a virtue
Amen no longer ending prayers
Talk the talk and walk the walk
Heaven needs our help to build the stairs

Living in the Son

Love thy God and love thy neighbour
Instructions left so long ago
Valid in the past and present
Information you should know
Named Jesus son of Mary
God's son was born with blood and bone

Influential from that moment
Navigating his way home

Teaching all to live believing
Heaven hears you when you pray
Exemplar of eternal living

Sage to saviour he displayed
On the cross he asked forgiveness
Not for him but those who strayed

Mantra

Manifesting every moment
Affirmation to be whole
Needs are met
The path is set
Reach for desired goals
Atonement for the soul

Mass Consciousness

Maintenance of mindset now required
Attitude does simply need to change
Selflessness promoted and inspired
Selfishness encouraged to refrain
Conscious effort needed to survive
Oppression be historic and take blame
Navigate to absolutely live in love
Sacrifice the ego and remain

Compassion for humanity desired
Indifference best described as inhumane
Options now for all to heal and pray
United by all living seeking same
Self-realise and recognise the greed
No jealousy or envy seeking gain
Existence is the reason to align
Step in line and find mankind is taking aim
Save man in time and in time save loves flame

Merry Christmas

May you be gifted being present
Enjoy the peace it brings within
Recognise to realise
Real eyes recognise you've wings
Yuletide starts the festive season

Christmas celebrates it's King
Holy days are marked for holidays
Receptive love on offering
Illuminated by divine light
St. Nick's soldiers dressed as him
Tis the season to be jolly
Merry Christmas people sing
Allow your light to shine for others
Share in all that Christmas brings

Mystical Poetry

Manifest every moment
Yield all that you've sown
Spiritual karma
Theology known
Immortal as farmers
Cultivating life's truths
Absolute comprehension
Loving all that you do

Positive perspective
Options for use
Eternal direction
Tactical truce
Realistic go forward
Yours to use if you choose

Mysticism

Mindful of your mindset
Your amazing innermost
Spirit strong here and supportive
Thanks to God for the Holy Ghost
Insightful and enlightening
Contemplating the divine
Intuitive and delightful
Soulfully sublime
Manifesting masterminds

Never Alone

Nurture your spirit
Exist with your soul
Value your conscience
Eternal your goal
Raise your vibration

Alone you won't be
Let go and let God
Oneness perceived
Never ever feel lonely
Embrace this belief

No Fear

Necessary for progress
Override fearful thought

Founded only by worry
Eradicate and abort
Abolish this mindset
Resilience retaught

Nothing but Love

No need to beg forgiveness
Own your life here and your sins
Take a good look in the mirror
Have a cheeky little grin
If you look a little deeper
Name your worth here and dive in
Guilt you hold here can be pardoned

But you'll need the love of him
Unconditional love on offer
Truth reflected from within

Love is the essence that you carry
Offered to your soul to bring
Valued far beyond your being
Eternal love requires wings

Oh My God

Overcome with mixed emotions
Humanity has failed

Mindsets fixed on money
Your garden struggles to inhale

God I call for intervention
On my knees I pray
Deliver us a better way

Oh when the Saints

Open are the gates to heaven
Holy art thou come and go

Wanderers of the eternal
Halo's on and on on show
Entry granted into heaven
No entry in is self-imposed

Transcendental beings
Healing hearts all unopposed
Entering and here in numbers

Soldiers soldiering composed
Aligned to bring alignment
Insync as one to show what's known
Navigate the way to heaven
Time for Eden to be shown
Shown the way to be hallowed

One Voice

Opportunity is knocking
Note that nothing is for sale
Eternal can't be bought

Value counts upon your tale
Open hearts will hear the calling
It's your inner voice that calls
Conscientious living
Eternal knowledge for us all

Oneness

Organised by feelings
Noble pass to be enrolled
Eternal is the knowledge
Next dimension is the goal
Enchanting whilst enlightened
Spirit plays a vital role
Slaying ego from the soul

Open Prayer

Open always for business
Prayers don't work if shut down
Express your prayers without endings
No greed in prayers is profound

Praise be given if answered
Remember Spirit's around
Amens best used for transcending
Your efforts light up your crown
Expect these prayers to be answered
Respecting prayers while earthbound

Parable For Peace

Present yourself as being present
Afford yourself to self-realise
Realise the wars are all-around you
Allow yourself to turn inside
Begin a peaceful inner journey
Learn to leave all wars behind
Eventually you'll get there

Follow feelings that feel right
Open your heart to forgiveness
Receive this gift of great insight

Praise heaven on your journey
Eternal soul you're now in flight
Advance within toward the heavens
Commandments written are your guides
Enlighten others on your journey asking why

Peace Perceived

Pass the baton to the children
End the war and cease the blame
Advance as planned as mankind
Claim this victory with good aim
Each and every soul here equal

Peace perceived without the pain
Egalitarian is the order
Righteous living and humane
Champion the people
Express to love as one again
Institutions re-established
Values gifted for man's gain
Elimination of indifference
Denouncing greed will change the game

Patience

Practice this virtue often
Apply it to all things in life
Take a deep breath as required
Immediately recognise
Everything is meant to be
Now's the time to think twice
Conscious of creating next
Exorcising lack of light

Prophetic and Profound

Poured from soul aligned with spirit
Rhymes here scribed upon the scroll
Omnipresent represented
Prophetic verse for all ye told
Heaven sent to vent his message
Eternal flame again near cold
Tell the truth and beg for pardon
Ignite the flame with faith to solve
Could it be made any clearer

Allow the flame to light the way
Navigation back to heaven
Done with kind deeds everyday

Prepare yourselves for when you're dying
Ready you'll need to be to race
Only difference is the rules are his
First and second here don't place
Oneness is the only winner
Uttered words here from his grace
No other message more important
Direct yourselves to live in faith

Religion

Rules rewritten through the ages
Embellishment of truth
Lessons sought and bought and taught
Institutional abuse
Genocide and conflict
Indoctrination of the youth
Occult like divisive doctrine
Non-inclusive poor excuse

Rest in Peace

Rest assured you're dying
Expiry date remains unknown
Sanctify your life whilst living
This means living to atone

Inspire those known around you
Nonchalant your faith displayed

Patience is by far best practice
Enlightened you'll portray
Act accordingly each moment
Count your blessings on the way
End your life in peace one day

Resurrection

Rise inside with self-assurance
Establish life again in light
Subscribe to be enlightened
Use your faith here to find flight
Resurrection of your spirit
Rise above and go beyond
Effort here is needed
Choose the path back where you're from
Transcendental being
Incarnate and out in space
Offer thanks and praise to heaven
Navigate there with good grace

Sacrifice

Silver spoon service
Aristocratic new way
Choices made in heaven
Receiving players play
Intrinsic your position
Fundamental this array
It's time to share with mankind
Common sense now on display
Ease in and gift away

Salvation

Subjugation diminished
Ascension from sin
Love is the answer
Validate and begin
Assemble believers
Transcendental akin
Instinctively align
One by one stepping in
Nothing left but to win

Spirit

Selfless and supportive
Psychologically sound
Inspirationally savvy
Righteous all-round
Intuitive guidance
Translation's profound

Spirit Fills the Void

Suffer less with spirit present
Peace within can then unfold
It's a journey to alignment
Roads ahead have been foretold
Invite your soul to soft surrender
Think of this space filled with grace

Flow as one again toward the end
I for one have filled this space
Listen to the inner whispers
Learn to block unneeded noise
Soul and spirit sync in silence

Talk from heart to hear his voice
Heaven's help is here on offer
Embark to fill this void for free

Venture forth as one together
Overflow with love the key
It's your spirit being spirit
Develop this as human being

Spirit Level

Saints have sinned whilst living
Personified are Saints as whole
Irrespective of the details
Rest in peace they could control
It is part of humans being
Taking steps towards the Lord

Live in light to be forgiven
Ego slayed is by your sword
Valiant you'll be in this conquest
Elevated is your soul
Leaving breadcrumbs on the scroll

Spiritual Growth

Some lives you've left behind you
Paths you've flown remain unknown
Incremental is your progress
Rights to enter yours to own
Insightfully enlightening
Think about this when alone
Use this knowledge on your journey
All on-board will turn to bone
Lead the meek and be a beacon

Guide those wanting to atone
Respect all others on their journey
Offer friendship as you roam
Want for nothing more than entry
Then comes the knowledge where you've flown
Heaven sees you on its path and walking home

See Beyond the Shadow

Seeing business ties as serpents
Elitists running politics
Egocentrics on high horse's

Bewitching lies and other tricks
Educators dulling children
Youngest adults buying bricks
Observing all that makes man greedy
Nourished selling tock's and tick's
Darkest souls stay in the shadows

There they sway without ethics
Heaven isn't on their radar
Every one of them is sick

Save for souls who seek eternal
Heavy is their crucifix
Awake and casting shadows
Drawn to light and here transfixed
Offer thanks and praise to heaven
Warmed by light the soul is fixed

Stand Firm (i)

Surrender to your higher self
Take a stand to advance if you do
Address the elephant in the room
Navigate with your free will to choose
Deviation from here creates chaos

Feel your way back to your feelings felt true
Insight is within and delightful
Rewards are eternal if true
Make each step about finding you

Stand Firm (ii)

Surrender to your higher self
Take a stance to advance if you do
A cross you will bear on this righteous path
Next step is to step into view
Don't take this path as for granted

Feel what you feel are your feelings felt true
Insightful is delightful
Rhymes from heaven channelled through
Manifesting footsteps to debut

Tap into Soul

Time it right to sense the timeless
Allow your inner thoughts to flow
Place your life into the hands of God

Inside your soul begins to glow
Name yourself as worthy
Truth be told to speak your truth
Open new paths in your journey

Solve the puzzled thoughts of youth
Onwards towards tomorrow
Unstoppable it would seem
Learn to live in all you dream

The Antidote

Throw away your false bravado
Heal yourself with dignity
Express your willingness for wellness

Awaken to our need for bees
No want or need for excess
Thank the earth for air we breathe
It's humility you're missing
Dose on this to help you see
Overdose is even better
Take a double dose it's free
Eden needs mankind at ease

The Sacrifice

There is no greater gift than free will
Hand your reins to God to steer
Eternal living is on offer

Salvation sought whilst living here
Archaic is this wisdom
Christ himself a sacrifice
Resurrect your soul whilst living
Immerse yourself into this life
Find favour in forgiveness
Indifference all but disappears
Compassion is by far best practice
Endearing soul to pioneer

Threading the Camel

Together is the answer
Heaven's gates are open wide
Recount your life upon arrival
Every soul shall go inside
Advance toward the judgement chamber
Decide if you'll depart or rise
Invest in this whilst living
Navigate this whilst alive
Guarantee your place in heaven

Think this through if you're to stay
Humanity needs healing
Enlightening others lights the way

Collecting all resources needed
Accumulate a commonwealth
Make it clear it's not for profit
Expand across all lands by stealth
Love as one to enter heaven in good health

Transcending Life

Take a hard look at your present
Reset your will to rise above
Authorise another lesson
New lessons learning love
Sacrifice contentment
Climb above until beyond
Eclipse your known potential
Nonchalant you should respond
Direct your soul to heaven
It's with grace that heaven calls
Navigate your path enlightened
God is there in case you fall

Learn to live with deep devotion
Inner journey through your heart
Face off with sin and remove within
Every lesson ends at a start

Transformation

Transcendental understanding
Rhyme with reason just to be
Awaken to your present
Nothing locked and thus no key
Spirit doesn't know religion
Faith within is all you need
Oneness is your destination
Reach here knowingly no greed
Manifesting magic moments
Affirmations guiding thee
Thank your spirit when enlightened
Instinct drives your quest to seek
Onwards to your purpose
Navigate and guide the meek

Transmit the Truth

Talk is cheap without the actions
Realise it's you who runs the show
Answer every inner question
Never lie within to know
Speak out loud within in silence
Meditate to gain control
Information is exchanged here
Trek to heaven is your goal

Take every new step willing
Heal yourself or pay the toll
Expect to judge yourself on entry

Trepidation for some souls
Rise inside if you are worthy
Use this knowledge growing old
Telling lies within won't get you in
Heaven knows you've now been told

Unconditional Love

Universally I'm present
Name you price for me to stay
Capture me with loving thoughts
Offer God your thanks and praise
Nothing else is wanted
Don't let pride get in your way
Intentions are projected thoughts
This way is how we sway
I am here for loving guidance
Only love can help me stay
Nothing else is needed
All other ways will see me fade
Love me deeply with your heart and soul

Love believed is a serenade
Open up your heart to heal
Virtuous being on display
Eternity's ours again

Unreservedly Eternal

Unlock your inner mystic
No religion is required
Righteous living is this journey
Enchanted is yourself realised
Spirit strong and ever present
Eternal flame alight and bright
Receiving messages from heaven
Vested interest in the light
End the search and claim your halo
Decoding life to live divine
Loving always and forever
You're in flight and right on time

Eternities before you
Take each step now wide awake
Every moment begs a lesson
Right or wrongly you partake
Navigate each moment wisely
At the end you'll weigh mistakes
Live eternal whilst alive and raise the stakes

Vibrations

Veils do lift slowly
Indicative of time
Balance brought forth in silence
Revelation in this rhyme
Answering a question
Till clocks tick a final chime
I for one am one for all
Oneness knows no one sublime
Nature does this freely without effort
Simple ways to be and shine

Wake Up

Whispering action
Awaken and breathe
Know it's ok
Egalitarian dreams

Utopian mindset
People in need

What would God do

Would he applaud the greedy
Have you given this a thought
Ask if you were in his shoes
Think he might just be distraught

Would he want for the destruction
Or do you think that he'd be pleased
Use your installed moral compass
Let your thoughts be based on he's
Do you think he'd be forgiving

Gods not the one who lets you through
Outdated if you think like this
Do what's right and think renewed

Do what God would do
Open gates depend on you

Will You Stand Beside Me

Where've you been whilst I'm waiting
I have God's gift to care
Love to rekindle
Life of knowledge to share

You are you and you only
Others must meet you there
Understand stand beside me

Surrender what holds your stare
Take a look in the mirror
And see what I see
New life you can live
Deep inside you can be

Believe in yourself
End this reflection of grief
Stand tall and deliver
I'm beside you indeed
Don't ever surrender
Etched in time to be free

Might you love yourself first
Expect life eternally

Wing and a Prayer

Will your weary soul awaken
Intentions true and from the heart
No need to turn for others
God has granted each their path

Advance with strong conviction
Nothing is standing in your way
Divine is your destination

Approach for landing at the gates

Pay penance on arrival
Recount the lessons that you learnt
Ascended soul in heaven
Your bones now buried and or burnt
Eternity awaits you
Receive the karma here you earned

Wisdom

Want to know a secret
intuitively it's known
Selfless self-awareness
Deconstruct what you've been shown
Open up your heart with kindness
Moral compass guides you home

Witnessing You

Watch your thoughts closely
Inner you to review
Tune into your being
Next step is renew
Expect split from ego
Separating you in two
Slowly you'll awaken
Imagine knowing who are you
No longer second guessing
Gaining ground on being true

Your ego will start hiding
Only option is subdue
Use your heart to see it through

Yes or No

Yes is one way of deciding
Equally you could say no
Sit on the fence if undecided

Or say nothing and stay low
Right or wrong you'll have an answer

Name and shame or kiss and go
Only offer your true answer if you know

CHAPTER 2: GREED

Alternative World

Altruistic mindset
Let go of alone to succeed
Think only of needs that will nourish
Elimination of thoughts thinking greed
Realise this world is worth saving
Nations peoples free willing to come
Accounted are all souls whilst living
Take stock and become now as one
Institutions restructuring easy
Vulnerable souls will still need us to care
Empathy rising for mankind

Worldwide and wide eyed we should share
Onboarding and leaving the cycle
Reincarnating for karma believed
Let go of all fear whilst you're breathing
Done right and each life is a breeze

Attraction

Affirming affirmations
Thank God and give praise
Think into being
Receive and amaze
Articulate preference
Create and enjoy
Tap into privilege
Incarnate and rejoice
Options are endless
Needs only by choice

Bet your Bottom dollar

Back your soul within whilst living
Eternal life is at the end
Training is required

You're here to learn and then ascend
Odds are locked and in your favour
Unite with Spirit here to strive
Request your needs be sent from heaven

Before you know it they'll arrive
Offer thanks upon receiving
Trust that heaven works both ways
To reciprocate is priceless
Offer heaven selfless days
Manifest a life worth living

Don't get greedy or seek fame
On a fast track back to heaven
Lay one bet on your endgame
Leave this world one day a winner
Atone your soul whilst here from sin
Run your race eternal living and begin

Bottom Dollar

Bet your bottom dollar
Owning money won't buy love
Trillions cannot buy it
Thousands spent can't rise above
One dollar trips temptation
Millions dream this sum and some

Dream of peace instead of money
Offer love and all will come
Leave behind what makes them greedy
Let it bleed away till done
Align yourself with your eternal
Raise your vibe without this one

Boundaries

Balanced by feelings
On with the show
Useless to turn
No need to go
Deny fruitless access
Approve only needs
Restrictions apply
If it's in its indeed
Emphasise your position
Show the world how to be

Celebrity

Captured till their crucified
Endorsed until their shamed
Loved and loathed and criticised
Egos stroked and egos tamed
Beauty shown rarely on the inside
Reality shows them mostly vain
Inherently attractive
Televised is soon to wane
YouTube claims the climb to fame

Consumption

Catastrophically on the brink
Off course assumed to fail
Not long before it's rations
Survival seeds betrayal
United Nations sanctions
Mandating laws without detail
Population not the cause
Think greed the truth prevailed
It's common sense to fix this
Only use what we need to inhale
No longer let greed be for sale

Corrosive

Caution if you go there
Only go there short to save
Reapers are resistant
Ravaged souls will hide away
Offer each their halo
Show both hands to pray
Instinctive they will follow
Very few will choose to stay
Exit quickly light the way

Constant Narrative

Conceptualise existence
On a path toward the Lord
Navigate toward the highest
Step by step to gain reward
Trouble's all but left behind you
Affirm your will to stay the course
Now you're living in the moment
Take every step without remorse

No looking back is needed
Aim your sights and feel your way
Rise up daily to the challenge
Righteous being on display
Adam's brother in the garden
Talking truth by telling tales
Imagine living reimagined
Veiled eyes no longer veiled
End this story to prevail

Devil in the Details

Devotees to heaven
Embody spirit by thy soul
Veiled truth now all but lifted
Immerse oneself with this thy goal
Love thyself and ye shall prosper

Incur God's wrath if you're to stray
No way back if you continue

The path is lit and it's one way
Heed this warning as if gospel
Embrace the rules thou shall obey

Deception past this point is deadly
Exalt thy soul or face decay
Time is ticking on your being
Action call to those awake
Involve thyself best by example
Lead the meek for goodness's sake
Saints and sinners all but winners at the gates

Desensitised

Disposition cantered
Every soul awake holds dear
Sensitivities depleted
Every soul awake sincere
Nonchalantly waking others
Seems to be the fastest gear
In denial most religions
Teaching fruitless faith and fear
Institutional propaganda
Selfless souls opposing here
Education sold and lying
Disrespectful of the sphere

Detachment

Disrupt the illusion
Envisage your worth
Things come and go
Accept and rebirth
Channel your spirit
Hold faith tightly and be
Manifest in each moment
Eternity's free
Needs come in alignment
Teach your heart to believe

Ego

Evil at its root
Grotesque at its core
Oblivious to lives law

Eliminate the Ego

Expect to meet resistance
Let your being find resolve
Intensions must be pure
Mindful of the ego's hold
Invest in your soul's purpose
Nurture this to resync in
Attachments feed the ego
Think this through and then begin
Eliminate the ego

Turn within and inward stay
Half a cup is now enough
Eternal soul within awakes

Ego soon falls by the wayside
Gone for good and gone it stays
On a one-way path to heaven keeping faith

Fancy Dress

Financials fuel egos
An assemblage of the mask
Narcissistic costume party
Classified by class and task
You know when you're invited

Dressing rules will be spelt out
Regulating your attire
Evening wear or thereabout
Serendipity might be there
Selfless soul best dressed no doubt

Fear

Found across all feelings
Especially that of loss
All-consuming nonsense
Remove it at all costs

Feeling Naked

Frivolous and futile
Existentially spent
Eden's been raped
Lament now the end
Industries spewing
Nothing spares their intent
Greed sees them gratified

No excuse for contempt
All but awaken
Know you're in need
End this self-satisfaction
Do what's right to succeed

Fertility

Finish line approaching
Extinction of mankind
Reproduction efforts futile
Termination of bloodlines
Ill-conceived are planned evaders
Left alive but left behind
In a duel with Mother Nature
Time will ring its final chime
You all here on borrowed time

Fragile

Frail our existence
Rest not a lot to save
Again please read the last line
God sent us not to slave
Intuition be your guidance
Love as one awake and crave
Existence is this way

Global Warming

Giant whales migrate the ocean
Life cycles plankton in the sea
Out of depth and hard to fathom
Balance bound to harmony
As are we amongst the challenge
Lies fly and feed unbalanced need

Warning If this goes unchallenged
Air up there will have no bees
Rumour has it without honey
Mother earth will cease to breathe
Inhospitable and barren
Now is the time for broad belief
God please assist let's guide the meek

Greed

Gather only what's needed
Reason indeed
Endangered existence
Existence in need
Don't be deceived

Guilt

Got a secret
Understand it's in you
Insurmountable it seems
Let it go and renew
Tell yourself sorry too

Haters

Harmony disrupted
Anticipated is this foe
Tactics needed for alignment
Exchange of love instead of blows
Radicalised will be resistant
Spirit is the star on show

Hierarchy

Hands up if you're good at this
Indicate if you're good at that
Every one of us adds value
Rewards are back on track
Achieve without deception
Results provide the facts
Cheaters cannot prosper
Hierarchy charged to act
Youth to front and aged to back

High Society

Humbled and inspired
I've a gift I must share
Guaranteed to satisfy
Humanity to spare

Social salvation
Ordained in deep prayer
Contoured equality
Institutions repaired
Exalted consulted
Taken in with due care
You're needed and recognised there

Highly Strung

Help yourself to ease your worries
Introspection yours to choose
Grant yourself the gift of courage
Heal yourself from your abuse
Let go of all the angst you carry
You're still sleeping and confused

Simply put You must awaken
Take a chance and seek your truth
Rise above your fear of failure
Understand this is your cue
No longer feel so unassured
Go forth and back the better you

Hunger

Humanities disaster
Unified fall from grace
Not meeting needs is culpable
Generational disgrace
Enough is enough for many
Rationally ration our race

I Kill Egos

Ignorance dismissive

Knowledge in this rhyme
I kill egos
Leave none behind
Lead by example

Evolution of the mind
Going going gone
On to universal time
Saints and sinners can both shine

Ignorance

Information worth sharing
Greed deemed a sin
Nowhere to hide
Opt out or opt in
Resign to alliance
Atonement begins
Needs only needed
Communities win
Each to their own discipline

Indifference

If you're good at making money
Name your worth to feed the world
Don't ignore those that have less than you
It's causing death to boys and girls
Feed them if their hungry
Find a way to share reward
Expect good karma for yourself
Respect all other beings onboard
Eden has abundance
None should go without a need
Capitalists find your kindness
Expect your soul prepared to leave

Institutes

Insurance should be assurance
Not-for-profit should be banks
Savages of savings
Taking all they can no thanks
Indefinite and intrusive
Talking fools not talking frank
Undeniable deniers
Tripping egos oozing swank
Embezzling high-fliers
Structure true remove all rank

It's all your Fault

If you know it then you own it
Turn away or stand for change
Simple is this concept

All aboard should feel the shame
Look again at those with nothing
Loving living free from blame

Your values your perception
One for all or one for fame
Unified and universal
Reconcile refrain reclaim

Faith is free along the lit path
Absolution is this way
Unconditional loves your ticket
Lend a hand to those enslaved
Tell the world you're here to save

Lifting the Curse

Love for all is unconditional
Infinitely now aware
Faith in God to find forgiveness
Take a stand as man and care
Insync with moons and mother nature
No other things in life compare
God has gifted us our being

Thank him from the heart we share
Heart is so much more than beating
Echo's pulse throughout our lives

Continuous deliverance
Unassuming it survives
Romance resonates with rhythm
Starts and stops and stays alive
Eden's ours again as man to tend and thrive

Lost Soul

Light the path to spark interest
Offer guidance if asked
Show the way if they pray
Take their hand if it's dark

Salvations for seekers
One by one and then two
Universal location
Loves the only way through

Malnutrition

Malfunctioning as mankind
Allowing famine fed by war
Love is long lost and ignored here
No excuse and no reward
Universal time's upon us
Take the answers to the poor
Remove the need for hunger
It's starvation at its core
Think of those with plenty
I see them held up with applause
Only woken eyes can truly see
Negate the greed and need's restored

Mankind before Money

Me and you and mindset
Another dollar we can't save
Name your worth away from work
Know you wither as a slave
Invest in being equal
Neighbourhoods in this parade
Distribute knowledge freely

Banking karma as fair pay
Everyone encouraged
Follow me in faith and pray
Or continue in this game of sin
Rest in peace delayed
Eternally you'll regress

Mindfulness will see you saved
Onward to tomorrow
Needs be granted each new day
Eternal living whilst you're being
You're alive to show the way

Military

Millions spent to murder millions
Illegitimate its cause
Languishing conscience
Institutional flaws
Transcend 'ye old battalions
Apply to serve and to restore
Re-enlist as gifted peacekeepers
You'll begin to win earths war

No Guarantee

Name your price for waiting
Offers well above reserve

Gift yourself away to prosper
Universal is your worth
Add a touch of exponential
Rarest quality is free
An alternative to money
Notes and coins date history
Truest values in just being
Expressing truth and harmony
Elimination of the need to guarantee

No Rhyme or Reason

No depth to our thinking
Off course and hostile

Roaming aimlessly living
Halos dull and not in style
Yielding less and further dimming
Mankind lost and in denial
Each and every soul here spinning

Oppressed by rank and file
Reaffirming faiths the answer

Rekindling life's flame
Enlightened beings wear halos
Action needed to remain
Salvation comes to those not greedy
Oneness comes to those reclaimed
No less than everybody is to blame

Normality

Nothing and no one are normal
Observations of life
Revisions of lifestyle
Manifesting mostly strife
Alternative apparent
Let go of the reins
It's in your best interest
Take a leap of faith
You've your soul to reclaim

Option One

Offer God your free will
Put your life in his hands
Take this option each day
It's for man to advance
Only one option
Needed now without greed

Open your heart
Nothing more is in need
End the same way each day to succeed

Out of Touch

Oppressive and retarding
Unrelenting and unreal
Tyrannical and testing

Out of touch of how to feel
Frivolous and fruitless

Taking liberties away
Overzealous and outspoken
Using force and power plays
Chaotic and corruptive
Hear hear they cheer and raise their pay

Over One Hundred

One or two or three or few
Venture into who are you
Evolving as your time here pasts
Recognise you're finding truth

Open up cognition
Number one in gazillion views
Emit a different wavelength

Hundreds of millions here will stew
Use your time here as a timestamp
Nothing other than it's new
Distinctly conscientious
Ring alarms all ringing true
Education down for many
Down to replay and review

Pay Attention

Perceive beyond perception
Awoken soul compelled to care
Yesterday's now far away

Aware tomorrow's not yet there
Take this moment to be present
Think this through and you'll progress
Evaluate 'your' here and now
Nothing left to second guess
Traverse past trepidation
Insist on cleaning up the mess
On toward a better world
No need for greed or pettiness

Population

Planetary inhabitants
Oppressed and in denial
Poverty and conflict
Universally on trial
Losing love among the people
An effort just to smile
Take heed and feed if in need
Ignoring greed is vile
Open hearts will recognise
No greed is now in style

Poverty

Population peaking
Opportunity to heal
Vested interest in the masses
Empathetically surreal
Rationale devoid of reason
Turn and face the truth and feel
You'll need to pray before you kneel

Power (i)

Pardon those of privilege
Offer life as being worth more
Watch as some turn cut and run
Expect majority restored
Reset morals to adore

Power (ii)

Peace its true objective
Ownership of self
Wealthy try to buy it
Earning it is its true wealth
Recognise yourself

Resources

Regulate distribution
Equality reinstalled
Sensible conclusion
One for one and one for all
United resolution
Rise as one or risk the fall
Cataclysmic this illusion
Express requested overhaul
Save and share and cares the call

Respect what's real

Respect all without judging
Every person's on their path
Some are lost and some are lonely
Paths divide and some paths pass
Every now and then you'll see one
Caught in the corner of your eye
The fact is that their learning

Wish them well and say goodbye
Hope and pray they find safe passage
Advance yourself towards reward
Take your best step going forward
Simply put be self-assured

Real you are when you've no ego
Express that real is in demand
Align yourself with hearts in health
Love the betterment of man

Sapiens

Species lost and withered
Awaken from this race
Perilous your position
Inept to change your fate
Extinction premonition
Need now turn as one to save
Seek now as one the gate

Save the World

Share your worth in this vocation
Assist if your inclined
Value contribution
Extend yourself aligned

Together is the power
Helping others redefined
Earth's beings stand to prosper

Wisdom well applied worldwide
Offer sensible solutions
Reestablish views refined
Love unconditional is the answer
Does a question cross your mind

Seven Deadly

Souls seeking salvation
Eternal in tune
Vetting each moment
Ensuring truth
Nostalgic in spirit

Determined and true
Esoteric mindset
Admitted by few
Detrimental if chosen
Lust is one too
Your soul needs no clues to get through

Shame on You

Sharing is not in your makeup
Happy you are in your fame
Anything selfless you challenge
Manifest madness your game
Ego thinks it can hide in your shadow

Others other than you own the blame
Naive you have been in your lessons

You know better than best to lay claim
Options to choose are not many
Universal time soon chimes to shame

Societies

Slipping in an out of conscience
Organised by class and skill
Citywide to countryside
Illogic yet it's real
Environmental impact
Take all now and leave none till
Ironic when in context
Earthmoving earth to move landfill
Systemic is the loss of your free will

Subscribe

Simplified solution
Unite and provide
Basically back to basics
Stand aligned and beside
Congregations ready
Resources applied
In sync to think of many
Belligerents denied
Equality worldwide

Technology

Timings right to tell the masses
Eternal living is your quest
Channelled is this information
Heaven sanctioned this request
Not all are called to action
Oneness calls the very best
Leading all to be awakened
Optimised by one address
Google is by far the answer
YouTube and Facebook link if pressed

The Powers that be

Thank them for their contribution
Help them come to terms with love
Educate them here and now

Present to them inside above
Offer sense and self-forgiveness
Ways they've not or never known
Emphasise it's time to change
Reassure them heaven's home
Start the conversation

Take them from their comfort zone
Help them see the light within
Attract them back from where they've roamed
Together there's a chance

Best bet is bet you're not alone
End your days in Eden knowing you'll go home

Tick Tock

Time waits for no one
Its design will soon chime to its end
Christ's life and not death forged a restart
Keep the faith that time restarts again

Time is now and times right and eternal
Observing Christ's message Transcend
Compassion and love make us equal
Know in your heart life never ends

Tolerance

Tactical truce and alliance
Open your heart go within
Life as we know now defines us
Ending this fight of non-kin
Race no longer divides us
Ancestry no longer breeds sin
Nonsensical blame now behind us
Collectively we win
Existence now in let's begin

Ultimatum

Until you find your purpose
Love will mostly flow away
Trapped and feeling anxious
It's a choice you need to make
Make the most of every moment
Advance in life or face decay
Ticks and tocks of time have chimed
Universally you play
Make the most of every day

Water

Way down low you'll find it
Atmosphere it's there
Temperature defines it
Every drop now valued rare
Recommend it's time to share

Weekend

Watch while we wait
Everyday ticks and tocks
Experience delayed
Keeps you watching the clock
Endgame entertained
Not knowing it's not
Diminished are days full of rot

With or Without You

Waste not the present
Invitation anew
Take a step back
Halo on and see true

Open your heart
Recalibrate your view

Walk now beside me
In sync and renewed
Together all weather
Helping me helping you
Objective corrective
Unselfishly through
Transcending this ending

You know what to do
Orientation creation
Universal pursuit

CHAPTER 3: PURPOSE

Adaption

Actions speaking louder than words
Do you agree
Answer in your loudest voice
Put yourself out there to be
Take a leaf of faith to conquer
Insight is for belief
Offer questions answered
Name your price as free

Articulating Being

Ancient wisdom rising
Resurrected from the past
Transcendental being
Introspection unsurpassed
Consciously connected
Universally defined
Living life eternal
Acknowledging divine
Trekking back to heaven
Intentions good as God demands
Navigation past temptation
Guided by fifteen commands

Be the best whilst being human
Enlightened being on a quest
It's the best of being on offer
Nothing more and nothing less
God grants your being here by request

Artistic

Articulating reason
Rhymes prophetic and profound
Thoughts from the esoteric
Imagineering sounding sound
Soulful pioneering
Truth be told it is life found
I am persevering
Choice is yours to stay around

Awareness

Action needed
Welcome all
All aboard
Redeemable
Extreme belief
No more greed
Explainable
Spiritual
Sustainable

Band Together

Be and live believing
Antidotal for your soul
Navigate your life toward the light
Darkness has no grip or hold

Talk and take those lost around you
Offer comfort on the way
Gather tightly walk toward the light
Earn your karma on the way
The worst thing that could happen
Has to be you're free again
Expect others there remapping
Resist dark souls who wish to reign

Be

Bet you didn't know
Eternal is the show

Be Thankful

Blessed are the peacemakers
Endearing nature on display

Thanking heaven on their journey
Heaven sent their thanks and praise
Answers on the ready
Navigators of the way
Keepers of the truth
Faithful they portray
Unified in purpose
Leaders of the peace parade

Be your Best Self

Borrowed time you've chosen
Eden hosts the flightless free

You've chosen here for karma
Or you've been sent here to bleed
Use your heart to light your halo
Raise your spirit instantly

Blessed are those awakened
Eternal human beings being
Set your sights on one day leaving
Think this out eternally

Sacrifice the ego
Egos breathing here are thieves
Let the love of a God embrace you
Find your purpose seeking peace

Bridge of Knowledge

Bestowed upon the conscious
Realised beings here advance
Installed into the psyche
Divine design of God's own hands
God provides for new horizons
Enlighten Eden on command

On a fast track back to heaven
For goodness' sake and not by chance

Knowledge shared for understanding
Now it's time to build the stairs
Open man's heart to eternal
Want for nothing but to share
Leave behind the false illusion
Enter each day well aware
Dream it into being
Gift it to those in despair
Educate mankind to care

Build the Stairs

Bridge the void into the heavens
Use your innermost insight
It's your soul within inviting
Luring you to find the light
Dive within to gain the knowledge

This inner calling you can't fight
Heaven is this way I promise
Eternal flame yours to ignite

Steps you take are towards heaven
There is no fear and thus no fright
Allow yourself to be forgiven
Immerse yourself into your plight
Romance the thought of you succeeding
Staircase built to God's delight

Calibrate your Way

Choices here are crucial
Avoid all short-term gain
Let go of things you've wanted
If it's needed then retain
Be grateful when receiving
Reject temptation eases pain
Attract good karma to your soul
Time here stops and present reigns
Evaluate your progress

You'll learn to feel how feelings sway
Offer this with hope and guidance
Use your heart to light the way
Reflect on being eternal

Weigh it up and the choice is made
Alone was your arrival
You'll also leave alone one day

Care

Calm and collected
Actions without fear
Relish every caring moment
Empathy sincere

Challenge Reality

Catch yourself in each moment
Herald in change
Action is needed
Love lost is strange
Look deep within
Edge toward new
Next step is faith
God is in you
Eternity's present

Reality is now
Each to their own
Alluring allowed
Lead by example
Invite one or few
Take a breath and just be
You've a new you to pursue

Challenge Yourself

Call upon your inner spirit
Hail in your inner peace
Affirm each day awake brings progress
Learn to leave behind spent grief
Laugh out loud when your soul's tickled
Engage and bring presented change
No need to tolerate oppressors
Go about your goals and aim
Explore your inner epicenter

You've a God inside of thee
Own each moment finding treasure
Using faith with firm belief
Rest as often as required
Salvations yours and yours to keep
Elevate your soul with kindness
Light the path and lead the meek
Facilitate finding faith in God's mystique

Change the World

Can you see what I see
Halos waiting to be worn
Angels waken from your deep sleep
Navigators take true form
Gently shepherd now the lost sheep
Enter one by one as born

Thanking heaven for each heartbeat
Harmonised by rhythm sought
Empower legal process

Wrangle in new common law
Oppressors filibustered
Rules rewritten fair and sure
Live life in peace with plenty
Detonate the old-world war

Channeling

Conduit of reason
Heaven's message is for all
Angelic disposition
Necessary to the call
No ego is allowed here
Equality must be
Linguistics not an issue
Interpretations are to thee
Needing only faith for contact
Gifting guidance to be free

Character Revealed

Challenge all to surface
Hast is warranted to heal
Angelic disposition
Race is on and it's for real
Alarmed is to awaken
Calmly answer to the call
Take a breath and deeply feel her
Eden's calling one and all
Reverence to her magic

Reverence also to the Lord
Eden crafts her own eternal
Veils lift and show your score
Eternal is the journey
All aboard can rest assured
Level up for those committed
Every moment on record
Do your best to reap reward

Conceptualise

Create alongside me
Old ways anew
New ways aplenty
Commonsense to preview
Externalise new pathways
Perpetuate new views
Terminating old clock work
Universal chimes true
Affirmative action
Let it be and review
It's greed superseded
Sustainably true
Ending all greed is well overdue

Conditioned

Convoluted chaos
On course to fall
No bees and disease
Disaster for all
I'm awake and I'm waking
Take a good look with me
I'll write what is written
On the wall it says be
No this is not cryptic
Each one looking will see
Deciphered to be sets you free

Conducting Life

Captivate the audience
Orchestrate the flow
Navigate the dance
Do your very best to show
Understanding purpose
Channel spirit as you go
Thank all and praise the heavens
Invest in healing hearts to grow
Numbers rise and numbers fall
Gatherers want to know

Leave them always with a parting gift
It's the gift of their halo
Free without conditions
Except for one. to make it glow

Competency

Creating a culture of caring
Organising of people for peace
Measuring wealth being modest
Practice in what's being preached
Enlightening only those asking
Tactfully teaching to teach
Establishing teams that are equal
Nominating team leaders for speech
Community-based and progressive
Yearly rewarded for reach

Cultivate

Commit to your life and be present
Unite to divide ye old spin
Live to love and laugh loud recommended
Take a deep breath and begin
Initiate sowing of no greed
Value words as the seeds you'll sow in
Activated by soul if inclusive
Toil this world free from sin
Eradicate greed from within

Direction of Life

Don't change direction
It's as simple as stop
Re-establish here and now
Eliminate the clock
Connect to your present
Take a step towards new
Instead of going around again
On a clock that's untrue
No concept of real-time

One of love and renew
Factual evolution

Learn your way through
Its design takes you around again
Familiar chaos your clue
Eternal living is waiting for you

Disclosure

Direction has been given
Information yours to share
Save yourselves is heavens message
Called to love and be prepared
Love is not to take for granted
Offer love when you're aware
Spread the love as you awaken
Unreserved you'll love to care
Radiate with warmth and kindness
Eradicate despair

Discovery

Dancing through dimensions
Investigating truths
Soul seeking sanctity
Consciously acute
Optimistic outlook
Vow to be astute
Eternal is the journey
Reincarnate absolute
Yesteryear's resolve is resolute

Distribute

Divide as required
Independent of creed
Share in the light
Thank all sharing need
Righteous done right
Invaluable deed
Be wary of spite
Understand greed
Take on this plight
Everyone needs a feed

Driving Lessons

Divinely enlightened
Roads ahead are all bright
Improve every moment
Veer always to right
Indicate your way forward
Navigations your plight
Gear up for romance

Love all day and night
Ease into the fast lane
Swerve only for shite
Slow down if you're lonely
Others drive in your light
No brakes in this lesson
Strap in and hold tight

Empower Others

Endearing nature
Mankind has a friend
Principal power
Ownership to all men
Wisdom endowed
Equality stance
Reach out

Outreach in defence
Talk loud
Help lend a hand
Empower
Respect and advance
Stand out

Energy

Expanding the heavens
Nourishing light
Euphoric its feeling
Realigns and ignites
Governing karma
You're a star shining bright

Existence

Earth bound for karmic choices
X marks your landing place
Instinct guides your seasons
Spiritually embraced
Take risk inside of reason
Expect amazing grace
No fear the risk of treason
Creation always procreates
Entries granted to these gates

Experience

Encountering moments
Xenophobes remiss
Perpetual soul
Eternal abyss
Romance the thought
Internal bliss
Euphoric when felt
Non-seekers will miss
Create being present
Experience this

Focused

Frequent to the frequency
Omnipresent and aware
Conscious of each moment
Universal Time declared
Spirit is projected
Eternities prepared
Designate an empty chair

Free Will

Faith affirmed by free will
Reverence to God's amazing ways
Enjoy the light when your time is right
Easiest way is to give God your reins

Wonder not the next step
It's as good as it gets
Love will come like a marching parade
Lead the band in demand keeping faith

Freedom

Find faith daily
Reaffirm right
Endeavor to be
Eternal the plight
Don't turn for others
Others will follow light
Manifest day and night

Fill in the Future

First thing is fix faith
It's the one thing you'll need
Let go of the past
Let the greedy one's be

Impress you are ready
Next step into view

Take a true leap of faith
Heaven sees truth in you
Express yourself freely

Faiths for all of mankind
Unlock the unlocked
Time to leave time behind
Unite with the needy
Remind those who care
Eden's our home and now under repair

Find your Purpose

Fortune tellers cannot tell you
Intuitives do not know
None other can answer
Destiny is your own show

You're your only best measure
Own yourself and just be
Use your own intuition
Reap and sow to receive

Place yourself front and center
Understand you're your seed
Reproduce when mature
Persevere to succeed
Oneness is your purpose
Secondary is to see
Eternity is living within thee

Footprints

Faith is the only fixed foundation
On a path traversed by few
One direction only
Take this path if you seek truth
Put your best foot forward always
Run or walk or stroll on through
It's not as easy as it seems
Nothing easy here to choose
Turning back is not an option
Spirit guides the soul in you

Foresight

Forgetting the moment
Often ends in dismay
Realising each moment
Entertains in the play
Sink it in to sync in
Insights this way
Go about your business
Harness today
Thank the heavens and pray

Frequency

Following feelings
Recognising right
Expectations are high
Quantum leap into light
Universal time chiming
End of this time in sight
Needing now always present
Consistent this plight
You're awake day and night

Genuine

Guessing games over
Egotistic you lose
Needing only the honest
Universal enthused
Instrumental in being
Nothing other than true
Exemplify you

Go the Distance

Get up and let's get moving
Other souls should see your heart

This race is just beginning
Humanity will soon restart
Established souls are needed

Direct mankind to shift and shine
Instruct them with your souls resolve
Strength to care and to be kind
This is not a lot I'm asking
Ask yourself what you would do
Now get off your arse and show your class
Come along and see this through
Eternal flame renewed in you

Going Forward

Gently awaken the sleepers
Offer your hand with a smile
Inform them they've not been forsaken
Nourish their light for a while
Gift them the gift you've been given

Faith in abundance for free
Open their mind to the mystic
Reverence to God to receive
Wake only those asking and ready
Action call to those willing awake
Redirect light on eternal
Do not be deceived by the snake

Greater Space

Gently you've arrived here
Roamed around and throughout space
Esoteric is your landscape
Articulating life with grace
Timeless and so timely
Exponential is your faith
Reliving time and time again

Spirit you embrace
Philosophical metaphysics
At an accelerated pace
Charging spirits wholly
Eternal lessons for this race

Here and Now

Hold your breath for a moment
Engage your self-controls
Remove yourself from autopilot
Energise your soul

Allow yourself to be your centre
Now you're back and realigned
Do this as you're manifesting

Now it's now you need to find
Open up and show you're grateful
Wide awake and right on time

Highest Order

Heaven sends Angels
Ideologically sound
Gifting all guidance
Helping all out
Enlighten all knowing
Spiritual clout
Transcending the meek

Objective is now
Resting to reap
Dissident's row
Embracing the present
Repairing by vow

House in Order

Honesty is policy
Opulence displaced
Understanding consequence
Stand beside the inner space
Eternal lives we're living

Incarnations in each race
Nothing tactile can go with you

Order nothing you can't take
Represent the meek with confidence
Defend their common faith
Egos will fall by the wayside
Ravaged by the hungry snake

Human Being

Heaven delivers
Unsure why you're here
Mankind in the billions
All living in fear
Numbers are needed

Be again one
Embrace the Orb Eden
In numbers you've come
Needing all and each other
Granted greed be undone

Human Capacity

Honesty shows reverence
Universal your wavelength
Mindfulness your magic
Aligned with heaven is your strength
Navigate each moment wisely

Call out greed that makes no sense
Advance once again as mankind
Pave the way without pretence
Act as one to claim awareness
Connect as one and all to flow
Indifference soon defeated
Take those asking where to go
You'll need to champion this show

I am Speaking to you

It's not about me

Absolutely it's you
My vision's for mankind

Speaking faith and the truth
Put yourself in the picture
Exquisite and rare
Ask yourself to the party
Know your worth's needed there
Incarnate and being
Now you need to tune in
Get over your ego

Take a stand and begin
Open your mind

Your eternal will thrive
Open your heart
Use it wise whilst alive

I'm here to Change the World

I'm manifesting every moment
Maps I've riddled through the rhymes

Helping others is a privilege
Eternal souls I wake to shine
Re-establish truth in being
Esoteric by design

Take a walk with me if willing
O'clock no longer needs to chime

Checkmate I say to players
Have you had enough of games
Are you sick of seeing sickness
Not even fame relieves the pain
Greed is slowly dying slowly
Eden's new age is to heal
The message is together
Healing gracefully is real
Eden needs us now united

Worry less when wide awake
Open to a new beginning
Resolving chaos and heartache
Learn to lift each other's spirit
Do what's right for goodness' sake

Identification

I know what I look like
Devoid of whom I truly am
Eternal is my being
Navigated here as planned
Trails tried and left behind me
Inch by inch affirming man
Finite living is this journey
Infinite my soul does span
Conscious of creation
Almighty God here in demand
Trepidation talks with truth
I recount truths you'll understand
On a side note We're both being
Neither of us can shake hands

Intentions (i)

Invested with interest
Negatives out
Think it out if required
Express aloud is allowed
Name your needs for alignment
To receive is to give
Inner passion with mindset
Own this life whilst you live
Nourish your soul if it's worthy
Seek to forgive

Intentions (ii)

Intellectual transmissions
Necessary they're sincere
Thoughts thought or spoken words
Essential that they're clear
No harm should be projected
This reflects upon you dear
It's a little like bad karma
Out of spite returns as fear
Needing only good intentions
Send out love and persevere

It takes its toll

Intentions here are crucial
Take all that's left and make it right

Think of all those lost and lonely
A beacon for them day and night
Keep meaning to move mountains
Exemplify what's kind and fair
Stay the course with faith and courage

Instrumental in repair
Time known only as eternal
Save yourself is by command

Take a hand if it's on offer
Offer your hand if you can
Let your soul rest as required
Lead the meek in saving man

Keep it Simple

Know to only take what's needed
Express true thanks for all you take
Enlightenment takes patience
Practise love for goodness' sake

Inch your way back home to heaven
The journey back requires faith

Sync with Spirit and pay homage
Intentions clear to pass the gates
Manifest and move man forward
Pray for others running late
Light the path for all who follow
Embark on being wide awake

Leading Edge

Leap of faith into feeling
Emotional flight
Answer the calling
Divine is your plight
Incarnated creator
Narrate and delight
Guide the lost and the lonely

Every word spoken right
Desiring tomorrow
Gifting back day and night
Equalities the quality of life

Lessons and Blessings

Learn from every given moment
End your days alive at peace
Simply put you live to die
Save your soul before release
On toward each morrow
Nine to five will cost you dear
Snakes here thrive from nine to five

Alarm bells toll and ring out fear
Now's the time to find true blessings
Define yourself awoke or sleep

Blessings yours to have and hold
Lessons learnt here are for keeps
Eternal rules are karmic
Sway your way and bide your time
Share in the Holy Spirit
Invest in other's souls to shine
New paths you'll make toward the gates
God has blessings here to find
Streamlining faith makes life divine

Let me in

Light now inundates you
Entertain the thought within
Time no longer dates you

Manifesting now begins
Externalise your wishes

In a manner you know wins
Negate thus choosing sin

Let's get Creative

Lessons learnt are many
Established souls in high regard
Testament to selfless being
Selfless beings on heavens guard

God sees that you are worthy
Express your thanks and send him praise
Take a stand and will you're ready

Co-create with God each day
Recreate in all his brilliance
Educate and show the way
Advocate to stay awoken
Tolerate who sleep enslaved
Innovate and get creative
Vibrate high and re-engage
Entertain like you're onstage

Life

Let it be
It gives and it takes
Fortune favours the brave
Exercised by mistakes

Look at your Life

Let's scratch below the surface
Others see only your display
Only you know you within you
Keeper of your truth contained

Admiration for your accolades
There are parts of you decayed

You're your judge and you're your jury
On the path back where you're made
Use this message on your journey
Repent if you have misbehaved

Light the way ahead for other's
It's up to them to feel their way
Feelings felt are forged for guidance
Each to their own still wills their fate

Manifested for You

Make no mistake I'm present
Absolutely here and true
No mistaking my intention
I am love and here for you
Feel me in your feminine
Etch this rhyme into your heart
Stretch your thoughts into the possible
Think it back unto the start
Endings started now and plausible
Death will one day loom on thee

Forever is your crucible
On offer is belief
Ringing true into your conscience

You've a true and willing heart
Onward to eternal
Universal masterclass

Moral Courage

Make a covenant with heaven
Openheartedness the deal
Raise your spirit from within
A life of living life for real
Learn to live in every moment

Conscious of the thought to feel
Offer truth and live-in love
Unlock your spirit to reveal
Rewards assured will afford many
Anticipate that some will sigh
God is the only one above
Etched in this rhyme is to abide

Mother

Miraculous in conception
Ornate in style with grace
Tremendous in her power
Heartfelt is her embrace
Evolutionary tenacious
Relentless in this race

Moving Forward

Monumental shift for mankind
Original sin to be resolved
Visualise a fair tomorrow
Insist it's fair for young and old
Non-negotiable agreements
Govern greed with guarantees

Forward thinking to the last time
Once again you'll be set free
Round you'll go until you're ready
When you're ready you'll seek thee
Allured by the mystique
Resolved to live eternally
Direction chosen is a choice and holds the key

My Free Will

Manifest your way out
Your gift is within you

Free your spirit to be
Resurrection of the truth
Eternity you will see
Exceptional and true

Will away your free will
Instincts will flow through
Live each day now knowing now
Loving life as God would do

Navigation

Nautical knowledge
Ark way back when
Valiant this conquest
Interstellar intent
Globalising guidance
All together again
Trip of a lifetime
Invite mind of man
Orbit aborted
Nirvana marks the end

New Dawn

Next chapter in existence
End the ways of greed for need
Wind down the want for wanting

Discover ways to supersede
Amortize said losses
Weigh up the need for all to feed
Name your worth here to succeed

No Regrets

Navigated to this moment
Over time has brought you here

Reflect upon the path you've travelled
Existing Pioneer
Galactic your position
Round and round you go
End this lifetime with good karma
Think of life as your own show
Share the wealth of all you know

Not A Soul

Neglecting one is not an option
Offer light to the darkest side
Thanks and faith is the instruction

Absolution you provide

Salvation is the path you're here for
Only follow me with pride
Use your intellect and heart space
Learn yours truly by my side

Optimisation

Overuse of this and that
Plenty fast becomes too few
Toll taken takes it toll on things
Imagine less if me or you
Man-made made a mess of man
It's greed if not renewed
Selflessness the Zen of life
Antidotal faith pursued
Take only what is needed
If it feels it's wrong refuse
Own the use of this and that
Nature navigates you through

Our Home

Outer reaches of the cosmos
Understand to look in and not out
Realisation you're in orbit

Heaven sent to turnaround
Offer knowledge of this to others
Make yourself and heaven proud
Eternal soul you're living now

Painting with Words

Picture what I'm writing
Artistic paintings drawn with words
Insightful and inviting
New ways to think of what's Inferred
Themes all constant and enlightening
It begs to reason the absurd
Narratively it's mastered
God willing that the words be heard

Will they whisper when reciting
Is it something man can use
Thoughts of pages framed upon a wall
Hung in plain sight for reviews

Will they touch the hearts of many
Or will they fade away with time
Rhymes I've written for the ages
Duplication the design
Share with care the words here rhyme

Parenting

Pleasurable process
Adaptation in play
Resilience is its brilliance
Endurance all the way
Nothing else really matters
Than a life you have made
Instinctively protected
Nurtured and named
God's gift that you proudly display

Permission Granted

Passage clear before thee
Entry granted at the gates
Rewards assured for kindness
Master days awake with grace
Immerse yourself in co-creation
Soar with Spirit as you fly
Synchronistic with the mystic
Immortal soul sought and realised
Opportunities await you
New paths flown so long ago

Go forth from here and prosper
Relight the flame within when shown
Answer only to your conscience
No fear here or foe is known
Take your time and smell the roses
Entertain all as you go
Divine design demystified and it's here on show

Personalities

Possession of the psyche
Egocentric and unreal
Relies on reassurance
Suppressing how you're born to feel
Our true selves feel us breathing
Nothing less than being true
Align yourself with mother nature
Learn your ego isn't you
It's a parasite you're hosting
Thieving bastard of your time
It's sad to see controlling others
Egotistically it climbs
Slippery slope for all mankind

Philosophically Present

Past and present paves the future
His story has and holds appeal
It's his history for the taking
Let your mind see mine for real
Observe the ones who are subservient
Sleepers walk asleep and slave
Oppressed and on the wrong path
Perhaps they'll wake before the grave
Humanity is broken
I see lives flicker and then fade
Calling one and all seems hopeless
All but one I've all but played
Let me take you on a journey
Let me show you how to pray
You're God's soldier when you're present

Pour out love and lead the way
Rise with me and find a purpose
Eternal flames shine bright again
Save yourself it says in scripture
Eternal living you'll attain
No better time than in the present
Time is ticking just the same

Pitch it to the People

Put your hand up to be counted
Insist together gives us more
Together we'll gain privilege
Count on numbers to be sure
Herald in the faithful willing

Identify where there are flaws
Take good counsel as required

Take your time to change the laws
Offer one and all safe passage

Turn all asking towards the Lord
Help all see the path they've chosen
Expect that some die by their sword

Peace here sought as God's agenda
End all wars is God's accord
On a one-way path to heaven
Peace if practiced is assured
Learn to love as one to get there
Eternal living whilst alive is the reward

Potent Potential

Put yourself into God's shoes
Observe mankind as self-absorbed
Turning a blind eye to the needy
Expecting others run the ball
Not now because you're busy
Think of those souls asking why

Perception is your power
Offer hope to those who cry
Touch them ever so gently
Ease the pain and show you care
Nurture those who ask for healing
Take the lead in how to share
Imagine man responding
Almighty mercy for us all
Lastly learn to hear his call

Present (i)

Proud and proficient
Reality is now
Eclecticism in vision
Selflessness vow
Exemplification
No need to show how
Tap intuition allowed

Present (ii)

Privileged to be here
Resumption of now
Entertaining perspective
Spiritual power
Ever so present
Negatives out
Turning within and show how

Present (iii)

Peace is found here
Reality seen
Existence has purpose
Sin is obscene
Everything's perfect
Needs known and in need
Take heed and fight greed

Present the Present

Perpetual gift
Restarting hearts
Enlist to exist
Show-stopping starts
Establishing moments
Nurturing next
Talking of love

Transmitting through text
Happens to happen
Eternal yet new

Presently present
Remembering you
Elaborate being
Sentient Soul
Entertain freely
No tickets sold
Time here stops to be told

Redesign

Round and round the garden
Environmentally bare
Devil in the detail
Eternally unaware
Seeds have been replanted
Instinctively regrown
Growing fast to everlast
No need to be resown

Refined Being

Refreshing rate is constant
Eternal life you live each day
Finding lives solutions
It's a life of lessons played
New steps present with progress
Each and every step on stage
Do what's right toward self-judgement

Beg for mercy if you've strayed
Enter heaven when you leave here
Insightful souls arrive to stay
Now you know you're living lessons
Get your game on and behave

Relight your Flame

Resurrect the soul within you
Evolve beyond blind faith and doubt
Lift yourself to be enlightened
Ignite your flame within if out
God uses this to stay connected
Heaven sees you by this light
This is your flame and it's eternal

Your soul is strongest shining bright
Only you can find your brilliance
Unlock your heart without restraint
Rekindle love whilst in the garden

Flaming hearts here reacquaint
Let your faithful heart define you
Awake to oneness without blame
Mankind is lost in fear and failing
Express fixed faith to share your flame

Remain Conscious

Ripped in two in review
Each side unaware
Mind games within
A lot to repair
It's the path to true being
New steps will find you

Conscious at all times
One-way back from two
No need for subconscious
Seek your soul to find one
Consciously living
In alignment to run
On board the Orb Eden
Use your time alive wise
Subconsciously die

Rhythm of Life

Romance the chance of being present
Honor each moment you awake
Yesterday entertained as now far away
Todays a new chance to partake
Honor thy God if you think to thank heaven
Manifest as you journey your path

Open your heart to God's rhythm
Facilitate in the lighting of dark

Let go of false hope and resistance
Indulge in the gifts you receive
Feel just as you were born to do
Eternal living you'll perceive

Say Thank You (i)

Simple recognition
Appreciation shown
Your spirit is listening

Think to thank to atone
Heaven sent is your message
Acknowledge this zone
Needed now is your faith
Know your never alone

You represent being
Owning your own
Use it wise before bone

Say Thank You (ii)

Salutations from heaven
Acknowledge Spirit is here
You are never alone

Thanking God is revered
How great thou art
Appreciations sincere
Needs addressed will manifest
Karmic and clear

Your requests are all answered
Only greed disappears
Unnecessary and dear

Screaming Soul

Silence for me is never golden
Calm my farm creates alarm
Relax a little's not an option
Easy does it holds no charm
Alarm bells ringing on the inside
Mankind is lost and doing harm
I struggle with man's silence
No leaders willing to disarm
God doesn't want this for us

Screams the soul inside of me
Our life is that of free will
Understand you chose to be
Lessons here are by decree

Shadow Known

Suffering the darkness
Humans doing inner war
Atrocities are rife here
Dragging knuckles on the floor
Overdue for lights transition
Wasting precious time in fear

Known for its oppressive hold
Now you need to simply see it clear
Overshadow goes your halo
Will it gone and by will it slayed
Nothing's left than a brighter way

Shadow Work

Self-realised gained through seeking
Hold faith tight to know your show
Allow yourself to sense you being
Discover depth that you should know
Operate as being eternal
Walk your way to reach this goal

Words are seeds that feed your journal
Oneness lets you read your scroll
Resonate with mother nature
Knowledge here will make you whole

Soul Science

Systematic knowledge
Observe your world within to learn
Understand the inner journey
Love yourself first your concern

Seek deep within for answers
Clues are hidden in plain sight
Investigate your feelings
Explore your core to find the light
New discoveries await you
Change of state grows wings within
Engage your soul within your being and begin

Soulful Sensation

Simplify your ways to reach here
On a pathway deep within
Use your fine-tuned inner wisdom
Let your true self here kick in
Flow of love is this sensation
Undeniable and strong
Love when full starts overflowing

Sense this feeling and move on
Emotions course throughout your body
Neck hairs stand upright on end
Sense your blood run as intended
A newfound feeling and old friend
Think beyond this as instinctive
It's so much more than fight or flight
Out of body but within you
Nirvana found within your light

Soulfully Being

Sold out or outstanding and ready
Old hat or old soul seeking truth
Useful or used and depleted
Lost in love or love lost your excuse
Find your way back to being though feelings
Understand it's your free will to choose
Learn to guide yourself back towards heaven
Let the kid from your youth be renewed
Yell inside out loud "please forgive me"

Believe in yourself through and through
Enlightened you'll be and eternal you'll see
It's the inside you need to pursue
Next step is to step into view
God granted the soul being you

Small Steps

Set your goal out in the distance
Mankind is worth the journey there
Along this path you'll feel emotions
Lessons here dismiss despair
Love and loss and deep devotions

Stand firm to step again prepared
Turn back for nothing and for no one
Exceptions at this point are rare
Practice patience as a virtue
Strides you'll soon be taking if you choose to share

Stand Alone

Self-discovery isn't lonely
This is the only path to wise
Allow yourself to be one and only
No fear is here and there's no lies
Discover deeper depth and substance

Anticipate you'll sync with soul
Loving you has one condition
Oneness comes to make you whole
No other one is needed
Eternal soul your life is solved

Sensitive

Sixth sense is inner feelings
Emotions unfold
No sense denying
Seventh senses hot and cold
Invoked and heightened
Trust eighth is just to be
It's the sense of being present
Vested and free
Empathy is nine in sensory

Take a Breath

Turn inside to find your essence
Archaic wisdoms in your soul
Keeper of eternal
Esoteric is your scroll

Allow yourself a reading

Belief is key to finding thee
Read between the lines you're reading
Every breath allows to be
Authoring your journey
Theatrical your style
Have another breath and smile

The Big Picture

Tap into you conscious
Have you seen what's just for you
Easy is your own big picture

Bigger is the one I view
I'm a challenge and I know it
Given this world is in despair

Please stand beside me
I'll do the hard yards
Consider me prepared
Thanks again my friends I'm worthy
United with you helps me share
Remember I'm the one who's risking
Easy for me if you care

The First Words

Theology finds the artist
Hell bound without a tour
Eternal is the journey

Fundamental faith and pure
Imagine life without us
Rise or risk is self-assured
Starve away the darkness
Think this through

We have matured
Offering the way home
Roads lit lead to the Lord
Dead ends are just diversions
Seek the light to gain rewards

The Gift of Giving

Throw your words unto the masses
Honour words you share as seeds
Every seed you share is fertile

Grow these seeds to ease disease
Insist it's time to weed the garden
Fruit is best grown in the light
Toil away till you've succeeded

Offer freely fruit that's ripe
Ferment the fruit that grows in excess

Gather often for the wine
Invite those looming in the shadows
Value all with care in-kind
Include the lost and disadvantaged
Name and shame those thieving seeds
God has gifted us these seeds to set us free

Therapy

Thank and praise your inner spirit
Heal yourself within life's show
Ease with ease into your being
Release yourself to be and grow
Accept some things are weird and mystic
Psychologically unknown
You're not alone from birth to bone

This is My Art

Tethered to heaven
Holy Spirit inspired
I am that I am
Scribing rhymes as required

It's a gift I do share
Salvation perceived

My message for all
Your halos are free

Alignment is needed
Righteous indeed
Take yours for a spin to succeed

This life is about You

Turn another year older
Happy birthday to you
Invest in your present
Sing-along for theirs too

Let go of the numbers
Inner soul to believe
Fact is that you'll die
End your life here at ease

Imagine eternal
Sense your life beyond known

Afforded only by faith
Build a bridge to this zone
Own this life past the numbers
Ultimate goal is to rise
Take a look in the mirror

You're a soul in disguise
On a jaw-dropping journey
Understand time here lies

Trailblazing

Truth be told it's cold and lonely
Right in amongst those who aren't there
Affirming faith with fixed direction
Inscriptions left to show all where
Leaving breadcrumbs back to heaven
Blazing pathways back to light
Letting go and letting God
Amazed to watch some taking flight
Zipping back and forth to set the course
Instructing all on board to pray
Navigating life eternal
God is willing all this way

Tune In

Thankful when you feel it
United with your soul
Navigate to go within
Entertain a common goal

Indifference disconnected
Network socially to solve

Turn around

Take a deep breath and close your eyes
Utilise your feelings deep inside
Realise all life is compromised
No time to blame and no time to cry

Advance again as man and realign
Run your race as if on borrowed time
Oppressions spent and set to leave behind
Understand step up and stand beside
New horizons needing your fresh eyes
Do it for God and do it to save mankind

Turn toward Being

Turn inward to your being
Unveil the mystical ways of past
Raise your awareness being mindful
No fear here with faith steadfast

Tune-in here to share in spirit
Open hearts here hear the call
Wonder here with love for living
Awaken here as one of all
Rise as wise each day with reason
Do your best each day to pray

Begin each day here being thankful
Eternal living is this way
Investing in your inner being
Navigate within without delay
God is within and he's here to stay

Unite

Universal is the mystic
Now is time to align
Identify your role in this
Time is now universal time
Expect this world to chime

What I Do

Warm our souls a little
Help us through
Attach a little of love
Think to say thank you

I don't ask for much

Damned if I do
Opening hearts I pursue

What is Art

Who dare define
Have you the inner mind
Adam and Eve to this were blind
Timed to tell

It even told time
Surreal it begins

A clock was designed
Resources each way matter as fact
Tick tock telling cost to mankind

What really Matters

Watching children die in war zones
Hunger killing more each day
Atrocities of mankind
Turn a blind eye look away

Religion's yearly wealth is trillions
Economic disarray
A completely broken system
Life only valued if you pay
Let's have a hard look at our present
You should feel sad if not ashamed

Making excuses is just petty
Accept that you accept this way
Trillions banked and children dying
Turn a blind eye look away
Every one of us is guilty
Remember this as we decay
Someday will be too late to pray

Who Are You

Who said you need a title
He or she or those or them
Opt-in and you've an ego

A life of living a pretense
Raise your spirit into oneness
Egos go without defense

You'll awaken to your beauty
Oneness shows there is no end
Universally you live and will again

Windows In

Watch where your eyes look
Incidentally how you feel
Notice something strange
Did you know that eyes reveal
Observations for the heavens
Windows watching through the soul
Sights are set to see solutions

It's how the heavens find resolve
Nothing veiled growing old

Words I've Written

Willing you awaken
Once upon a time in rhyme
Read every word with care
Destination is divine
Scripted straight into the conscience

I have a reason I've to share
Vested is my interest
Eternally I am prepared

Words written here are breadcrumbs
Resonating as designed
I offer this confession
The words I've written are not mine
These words I hear from heaven
Enchanting parables I scribe
Narratively the story screams it's time

CHAPTER 4:
HOPE

Abundance

Ample of what's needed
Bountiful and all around
Unlimited resources
Nature has our needs abound
Don't be deceived by dollars
Affluence by right dismissed
Not needed is old money
Count out greed and coexist
Entertain the thought of this

All Aboard

Accelerate your being
Leave your past behind
Let your future be with peace

Allow your inner self to shine
Believe and be your present
On board your souls divine
Attract good karma to yourself
Remind and mind your mind
Discover we're entwined

All we need is Hope

Awareness of the finish line
Leave the game of chance behind
Let those games be for the children

Whilst you're breathing you should shine
Everyone who counts accountable

None but you should count your name
Everyone who counts accountable
Express your worth or feel the shame
Destined for a higher calling

Invest in your eternal flame
Sync with ease into your spirit

Hope is here for you to claim
Onwards to less suffering
Peace is possible to obtain
End this false and fearful game

Beautifully Broken

Born to reach the heights of heaven
Enduring suffering for gain
A shipwreck full of hidden knowledge
Unrecovered and contained
Transition is the final mission
Intensive care your ball and chain
Forthright and fixed in your conviction
Unrelenting in your aim
Love has been learnt and is your pardon
Love for God within remains
Yesternight is now behind you

Break of day not far away
Remaining all so ever present
One loyal to the one who reigns
Kind and loving and so thankful
Epitomising keeping faith
Nothing is learnt unless you break along the way

Beautiful Soul

Beauty is your cosmic centre
Every one of us is love
Allow yourself to be connected
Underfoot is you above
Tantric the alignment
Inhale deep the breath of trees
Feel your spirit reconnecting
Unified with life at ease
Lose yourself into the mystic

Souls unfold in life resolved
Orbiting at God's speed
Unite your body with your soul
Learn to live in love the goal

Behind the Gates

Blessed are those who live there
Elevation highly sought within
Heaven's levels all have purpose
Incarnations there begin
Nothing needed there but free will
Divine designs are in great halls

The gates are always open
Heavens rules are known to all
Enter through the judgement chamber

Guardian angels are your guides
Assess the life you've finished living
Talk of deeds you've done and why
Ease yourself into the centre
Say thanks to all inside and rise

Behind the Mask

Bleeding hearts amount to many
Empathetic souls are more
Healing seems to be elusive
It's source unknown and man's unsure
Nothing like this in this lifetime
Death feels nigh and at the door

The game has changed again forever
History again records deaths score
Eden seems to be upon its knees

Man is scared yet fear is flawed
Advocate awake for goodness' sake
Seek within to find the Lord
Keep the faith till calms restored

Being Human

Before you sleep be thankful
Every time you wake give praise
Instrumental to reach oneness
No regretting yesterdays
Guarantee yourself salvation

Human being full of faith
Using wise your gift of free will
Make the most of living days
Amaze yourself by being present
No better option than this way

Believe It or Not

Boundaries well outside the physical
Eternity explained
Let go of all you thought you knew
Imagine living life this way
Everybody conscientious
Vibrations rise and field change
Entertain less suffering

Invest in karmic gain
Tolerance encouraged

Offer love instead of blame
Raise yourself above indifference

No longer feeling thoughts of shame
Only help those with their hand up
Take their hand and show the way

Breaking Hearts

Broadcasting are the angels
Reminding us to pray for real
Endangered is their message
Amazing grace again revealed
Kindness is within your conscience
It's understood that hearts must heal
None seem to hold true faith divinely
God got the raw end of the deal

He allows free will in Eden
Express your faith and praise his reign
Allow yourself to seek forgiveness
Right your wrongs and start again
Thank the angels who remind us
Show up with heart that beats humane

Broken Soul

Bravo you made it
Rightfully you've come this far
Outer corners of the cosmos
Know your soul's a shooting star
Every step you now take surely
Next steps to see the world renewed

Steps you'll take with faith and fortune
Other lives you've lived less true
Unencumbered soul you're ready
Leave behind the broken you

Celebrate Today

Can you guarantee tomorrow
Each and every day is rare
Living is a chance in billions
Expect to exit unaware
Breathtaking is so brilliant
Relying solely on fresh air
An almighty gift is living
Thank the heavens you're aware
Eden is your home and garden

Trekking throughout outer space
On an orbit in space spinning
Do you credit God's good grace
Another day you're living
You should really celebrate

Children

Choices made in light of heaven
Halo on to guide the way
Innocent beginnings
Living lessons learnt in play
Daydreaming in the present
Receivers on parade
Enlightened beings from heaven
Nurture this and Spirit stays

Coincidence

Culmination of vibrations
Obeying forces unrealized
Incomprehensible to fathom
Nothing less than feels alive
Chance remains the choice for reason
Intelligent design remains declined
Daylights dawn for those awakening
Evening's night and right on time
Needed only is perspective
Crowned by halos while they shine
Enlightened know to praise divine

Colour Blind

Capitalists bring chaos
Observe their overlords of war
Love is never their agenda
Owning worthless things adored
Unstoppable collectors
Rubble sits atop their rings

Blinded by their money
Loving only things it brings
Imagine what they want when dying
No less than heaven I am sure
Denied they'll be upon death's door

Connected

Contemplate existence
Observe your life is here and now
Next is always yet to happen
Nothing happens till you plough
Extract all negatives to center
Culminate as crowds allowed
Toil away each day with purpose
Exist as one of all and proud
Disallowing greed a vow

Conscience

Categorised crazy and classified sane
Outdated opinions
Nonsensical blame
Sanctimonious reasons
Consultations unpaid
Institutional treason
Ego displayed
Narcissistic empowered
Conditioned to frame
Each soul in this group will feel shame

Consistency

Character assassination
Own yourself with no blame
Next step is forgiveness
Set your sites on regain
Intangible interest
Saving self from insane
Taylor made mindset
Every soul thinking same
Narcissistic ecliptic
Creating creates
Your fate

Contemplate

Consideration always
Open heart and open mind
No sense of hopeless
Thank the divine
Exhaust every option
Master sublime
Perseverance practiced
Love all and be kind
Appreciation of spirit
Take on board a new time
Everything will be just fine

Cosmos

Can you truly fathom out there
Out in space and void of time
Stardust across the cosmos
Mars now reached by man's design
On the opposite trajectory
Stardust within you'll also find

Countdown

Count everyday a blessing
On board Eden your days end
Understand you're universal
Number days till you ascend
Take this on as your best option
Direct your soul to seek insight
Open up your heart to guide you
Wings within assist in flight
Navigate your way to heaven in this light

Created Evolution

Cosmic creation
Relative time
Express evolution
Accommodating mankind
Terraforming the surface
Eden ready to rear
Dinosaurs served their purpose

Extinction to clear
Vegetation delivered
Orbit set to renew
Lowest speed for survival
Universal time view
Thirteen moons in the cycle
In sync and sincere
Onboard toward tomorrow
No judgment or fear

Cycle has Closed

Clandestinely crafted
Ye old way is nigh
Crafted by the Grand Master
Lamenting what's right
Evolution in question

Halos again shining bright
Absolutely confusing
Soul searchers see light

Closed minds stay deluded
Lost souls in their plight
Others are cruising
Seeing love in their flight
Endurance endearing
Done day and done night

Darkness

Depressed and disillusioned
Anxiety set to rise
Restless as you spin again
Kaleidoscopic mind
Now it's time and Now's the answer
Every now you can make right
Select the best of every moment
Seeking out the path to light

Darkness Dawns

Direct your way out of the darkness
Advance your life toward the light
Reconcile your karma
Known as perilous is this plight
Not too many have succeeded
Even less have borne the cross
Soul searching is what's needed
Salvation seekers bear the cost

Delivered is the outcome
Awake to see and feel the pain
Wanting only for a better world
Nothing less than see God reign
Save man from sin and start again

Dream

Drift far into the lucid
Relaxation at its best
Esoteric this illusion
Absolution
Manifest

Deeply Connected

Direct your light toward the living
Eden is your world to save
Endangered is existence
People sleeping and enslaved
Love is lost amongst the living
You have a cross that you will bear

Carried with conviction
Once awake you'll sense despair
Not needed are the useless wants
Needed now is those who care
Every soul here is affected
Can't you see most things unfair
Take a leaf out of Christ's book
Earn your best karma there
Do your bit and commit to repair

Down the Rabbit Hole

Discoveries await you
Open doors explored before
Ways in and out have turnstiles
No doors locked are reassured

The end you think you'll come to
Have faith it never ends
Enchanting as your soul unfolds

Release your ego and pretence
Adapt as you awaken
Bring an open mind to see
Back yourself with your self-wealth
Imagine life eternally
Think the infinite you've journeyed

Hold on tight and enjoy the ride
Others need your help awaking
Let them see your love and light
Entertain your souls in flight

Dust to Dust

Delivered to learn lessons
Ultimate lessons learnt in love
Soul placement in the cosmos
Thoughts best inner than above

Terra firma forms our being
Onboard Eden with her Sun

Dimensional adventure
Universal time has come
Spiritual deliverance
Take your halo and succumb

Death

Dust to dust
Eternity's gate
Ashes to ashes
Theological fate
Hold on tight and have faith

Emotion

Etched into the psyche
Melodramatic if untrue
Overwhelming feelings
Touched with love or feeling blue
Intimate encounters
One on one or two or few
Navigation within you

Emotions

Everyone has feelings
Mood swings from love to pain
One's mental take on others
Translated in each brain
Intuition is your boundary
Open hearts present the same
No tolerance for suffering
Show antagonists in shame

Empathy Rising

Exponential human value
Motivated from the heart
Psychological attraction
Altruistic from the start
True-heartedness affection
Human natures drive to feel
Young and old receivers

Rising day by day to heal
Involuntary emotion
Selflessness portrayed
Instinctively connected
Natures empathic way
Gifting healing love away

Empty Chair

Everywhere I'm present
Maps to me devoid don't roam
Prayers help convalescing
Take a seat relax I'm home
Your life is now transparent

Cherish faith renowned and known
Hale your souls' objectives
Angels will rest here if shown
I am that I am represented
Reminiscent of my throne

Encouraged

Every dawn as you awaken
New questions form inside
Contemplation us the day unfolds
Observations through true eyes
Understanding consequence
Regulate to compromise
Agree to disagree with some
Given time they'll soon realise
Every dawn as you awaken
Demonstrate how to arise

Epilogue

Extending this life force
Peace be your friend
I am that I am
Let go of pretend
Oh my God are you kidding
Guard your time and defend
Use your heart now and realise
End no longer means end

Euphoria

Eve knew this in Eden
Unencumbered she failed
Present again
Historically scaled
Oneness represented
Redemption entails
I am that I am
Amazing this tale

Evolution

Existence was created
Variations in all life evolve
Opposition to either rejected
Look to faith for resolve
Universal time is present
Tap in and find life solved
Incremental in its progressive
Offer faith to warm the cold
New dimensions soon unfold

Exit Time

Eternity is present
X multiplies through
I am that I am
That I am

That is true
I am that I am
Manifested in you
Expect me to come at your exit time too

Fearless

Faith fixed for guidance
Every step taken sure
Aimed at alignment
Reassuring reward
Love in your corner
Eternal your flight
Soulful surrender
Spirit in flight

Feeling for Real

Feel straight through your heart
Exit your mind
Eliminate thought
Let your heart shine
Intimate feelings
No fear by design
Goosebumps and tingles

Faith here is divine
Opt out of judgement
Real you'll soon feel

Raise your vibration
Empathy is the deal
Align with your centre
Learn what feelings reveal

Find Me

Faith is not religion
Incessant ticks and tocks aren't time
Navigate to next is void of maps
Do you control your mind

Manifesting every moment
Eternity with me you'll find

Find the Beauty

Fix your focus to find beauty
Inspect with love reflectively
Nature Is your best example
Divine design here is the key

Tune in to master all your sensors
Heaven helps those who believe
Every breath you take is priceless

Breathe out freely for the trees
Every step you'll take enlightened
Allow yourself to walk at ease
Use this gift whilst you're out flying
Take another step and breathe
Your beauty lies within for all to see

Find the Positive

Finite resources
Insatiable greed
Nowhere to run
Dogmatic indeed

Take a fresh look
Have faith and find thee
Every soul owns a halo

Put yours on to proceed
One by one we'll awaken
Successions succeed
In perspective perception
True tenure in need
In being within
Vested right to accede
Each eternally free

Fire

Flaming Solution
Ignite with care
Restrain if required
Extinguish despair

Full Emotions

Faithfully I'm tearful
Universally I feel
Lovingly I'm loving
Letting God in to make it real

Emotionally I'm connected
Mindset is to forget I slave
Open minded to each moment
Take a leaf from JC and pave
I'm one of all and ready
Open heartedness displayed
No regrets as I feel for many
Set an example and lead the way

Go with the Flow

Galactic is your present
On a big blue ball in space

Warmed by a bigger ball that beams
Incarnation in this race
Third ball in in this equation
Has a calm affect at night

Take a pause and think about this
How the hell are you in flight
Exceeding speeds that you can't fathom

Flowing at speeds beyond your means
Let go of all the shit you carry
Open your heart to more extremes
Welcome to heaven human being

Goodwill Matters

Gift freely your well wishes
Offer goodwill prayers away
Open your heart to be giving
Do it night and do it day
Wish the best to all of mankind
Imagine love flooding their way
Let your heart burst overflowing
Learn to live for love again

Miracles happen daily
Allow this be front of mind
Telepathic kindness
Transmitting the divine
Energy sent that's positive
Radiating higher vibe
Spirits sharing in the light

Google Homepage

Graphs and charts of populace
Other charts of shame
Open links to each of these
Give an objective view not blame
Let all of us decide the course
Every human in this game

Humanity in all of us
Open up the page
May God be with you and good luck
Expect the one who reigns
Pay tribute to the ones in touch
Announce their victory and name
Give to souls that need it most
Exclude those who won't play

Grounded

Galactic your position
Reverberations for this earth
Open heart and open mind
Universal is your worth
No need for recognition
Don't expect advice
Expectations come and go
Done right once again and thrice

Happily Ever After

Have you thought about your ending
Are you even on your page
Put yourself into the picture
Pages written are like days
Indexing your emotions
Love and loss and days in rage
You're the author of your story

Every page is you on stage
Volumes all about you written
Every chapter you're the star
Reams and reams of you in writing

Authored dreams of who you are
Fair to say this isn't fiction
Tales you've written you can quote
End your story as pre-written
Rest in peace the author wrote

Heart Attack

Humanity needs you
Earth needs repair
Articulate reason
Reiterate rare
Take a stance for survival

Attract all with care
Take a heartfelt tactic
Talking reason to share
Affirmative action
Care for all in despair
Keeping heart in your prayer

History

Humanly present
Indicative of time
Semantic phonetics
Telepathic sublime
Ordained progressive
Retrospective defined
Yea old way is nigh

Homeward Bound

Home sweet home I'm coming
Open gates at heaven's door
Mindfulness whilst living
Eternal thoughts are reassured
Welcome my deliverance
Atoned my soul to stay as saved
Rest in peace from being
Delivered thrice before repaid

Blessed to live amongst the angels
Offer me a place to stay
Universally I've travelled
Need I stay another day
Dreams of home I'm on my way

Honesty

Honour and integrity
Objective is through
No need for deception
Eternally true
Straightforwardness matters
Truth will see you renewed
You and you only seek you

Human Spirit

Humanity rising
Unfolding in spades
Manifestations of many
Abundance of faith
Nuance of culture

Spirits commune
People waking together
Inner thoughts back in tune
Resurrection of spirit
It is me and it's you
Together we bloom

Humanism

Humanities front and centre
Understanding here and now
Mankind is lost and needs direction
Action needed to show how
Name yourself as one who's trying
Individuals will assist
Save this world for those tomorrow
Manifest to coexist

Humanity

Hollywood objective
Uniting through art
Mankind represented
An alliance of heart
Narration of treason
In a script to restart
Together the reason
You star in your part

Image

Imagine me naked
Make yourself naked too
Agree now we're equal
Gifted life to live true
Egos die to be you

In Times of Doubt

Intelligence seeks out reason
No fixed faith requires hope

The path to heaven we're all walking
It's your thoughts that sense a slope
Meaning sought to find your purpose
Endless doubt and guilt and shame
Stop this illusion with forgiveness

Only you can cease the blame
Fix your faith to balance reason

Doubt undoubtedly left behind
On path again toward the end
Use your faith to guide your mind
Belief is for believing
Think of faith as fixed Not blind

Instinct

Intuitive feelings
Neurologically known
Sensational sensors
Tangible tones
Intelligent tingles
Nose through to toes
Conscious communication
The whole body knows

It's not Rocket Science

It's a fundamental lesson
Thinking here and now till then
Sync with spirit and be present

Next you'll learn that life extends
Oneness shows up new horizons
Trail blazers in demand

Rocket science for the soul
Once in orbit there's no end
Count for times well after lift-off
Karma is your only load
Express you'll go into the heaven's
Taking with you this payload

Save whilst here this precious cargo
Collection doubles if sincere
Investing in your life eternal
Eternal living whilst you're here
No other knowledge needed
Calculations have been done
Exit Eden with good karma and you've won

It's Time

Intelligence should tell you
Timing time in time's insane
Second handed is your prison

Time to loosen off the reins
It's a little like religion
Manipulation of true faith
Eternal thoughts will see you true again

Lifetime

Lost you are but not forgotten
Incarnation became you
Feelings follow you through lifetimes
Eternal living is what you do
Time will tell again if willing
If it's willed you'll see this through
Master every living moment
Every moment living true

Listen Intently

Let go and let God
Internal you'll hear
Spirit calls from within
Tune in until clear
Everyone's a receiver
News old and sincere

Inaudible feelings
Naked soul to revere
Telepathy to centre
Emotions bring tears
Nothing ever comes easy
Tactful souls persevere
Let down your defences
You're your soul's engineer

Living Eternity

Live in love and laugh
It's lives lesson
Visualise all that you need
Invest in your life and be present
Navigate life free from greed
Gifted with guidance from heaven

Enlightenment offered for free
Thank heaven for all you are granted
Encourage mankind to now be
Rest only when peace is presented
No time left for this not to succeed
Irreversible is your transgression
Till death do us part whilst you bleed
Your purpose to reseed no greed

Moments

Magic if captured
Opportunity seized
Memories are made here
Evolutionary seeds
Nestled in faith
Tenacious indeed
Set to reset and to supersede

Nothingness

Next is not yet
Origin naught
Take none from none
Hold nothing in thought
Infinite empty
Never ending it seems
Goes on a long way
No in or between
Exponentially vast
Staggering extreme
Sacred space for new dreams

Now

Now's the time between tick and tock
Open your mind and stop the clock
Will you lead or will you flock

Nursery Rhyme

Nature needs us more than ever
Understand that we need bees
Round and round and round we go
Spinning roughly with disease
Every spin is one less dinner
Round and round and round we go
You'll get dizzy getting thinner

Racing faster going slow
Have a look to spot a sinner
You can see it's greed they need
Money here is not the winner
Expect your funeral flower free

Osmosis

Offering salvation
Sanctification of your soul
Mingling of your mindset
Outpour of love to make you whole
Simple is this sole solution
It's the subtle pass of love
Sink within to sync above

Out of this World

Once upon a time's your story
Use your time awake and wise
Think to thank the heavens

Open wide your veiled eyes
Fill the void you're feeling

Take a leap of faith and fly
Honesty is needed
It's the cornerstone of life
Seek to be enlightened

Will to obey and to abide
Observe you're universal
Round you go until you die
Let go of judgement and of ego
Devote your soul to heaven whilst alive

Over the Rainbow

Offer all your introspective
Volumes speak that you conceal
Expect to find within your richness
Resonate with vibes you feel

Truth is rumbling on the inside
Heaven knows your thunderous heart
Empathetic when it's storming

Repent for sins has played a part
Awareness of this is a God send
Inner strength must tear to heal
Naked soul perform a rain dance
Beyond the storm is life surreal
Only a flood of love will save man
Wide awake to life revealed

Premonition

Positives come from chaos
Reminiscent of times before
Egos strong and shooting arrows
Military misused for war
Offence is masked as defense
Non-discriminatory discord
Indifference plaguing mankind
Totalitarians onboard
It's my honest premonition
One day we'll turn as one assured
Next world order shares reward

Remember to Imagine

Realise you are creation
Evolution on the run
Make every moment count
Express your heart and soul as one
Miracles are made here
Blank canvas yours to paint
Every one of us creators
Roleplay sinner or play saint

Time here is not forever
On towards your final day

Imagine life without you
Memories of you on display
Align yourself with heaven
God will listen if you pray
Imagine life eternal
Now come back to life in play
Eternal living works this way

Rise and Shine

Representing mankind by example
Instruct that fairest take the lead
Souls seek to walk with souls awoken
Explore the scriptures of the meek

Angels assembling for guidance
News soon spreads quickly of belief
Don't turn for those who call from shadows

Self-saving wealth you will bequeath
Honour life as God enables
Insist that fighting is to cease
Next chapter ushers in forgiveness
Empty chair now symbols peace

Roller Coaster

Ride your days into each sunset
On this ride you know as life
Let go of expectations
Leave behind their said advice
Endurance here is needed
Round you'll go and pay the price

Concentrate on being
Offer nothing but be nice
Action here will speak the loudest
Spirit strong with faith restored
Think to thank the heavens
End this ride on your accord
Resurrection self-assured

Shine and Guide

Set your sails toward the heavens
Holy Ghost within to guide
Intrinsic is the mystic
No stone left unturned behind
Entertain the seeking masses

Articulating God's good grace
Navigate past fame and fortune
Direct your thanks to God with praise

Guarantee the destination
Universal time portrayed
Invest in being present
Do your damn best everyday
Enlighten others on the way

Shoot for a Star

Seek to find your brilliance
Hone this skill by aiming true
On board this orb called Eden
Observe that next is always new
Trajectory is perception

Far away or within view
Outer reaches on the inside
Reflect on who is finding who

Affirmations help you get there

Spirit known will help you too
Take good aim at every moment
Advance each moment if you do
Reach out for the star in you

Soul in Flight

Situated in the cosmos
Outer edges of the known
Universal understanding
Landing here is to atone

Incarnate as one with nature
Nature offers flesh and bone

Fornicate to procreate
Love is balance in this zone
Instinct will guide your purpose
Gift love to those alone
Heaven sent you with a message
Talk of the seed of no greed being sown

Soul Lost

Spiritual void
Oneness depleted
Universally spent
Lost and defeated

Loveless and lonely
On the path of despair
Spin within quick
Take your halo it's there

Suffer Less

Starve away temptation
Unhinge the thought of fear
Form the future step by step
Follow hearts that beat sincere
Endure the change that is needed
Release the past to free the pain

Let love be your reflection
Entertain the love you'll gain
See yourself one day in heaven
Seek your own eternal flame

Symphony

Stars dance throughout heaven
Your compass of time
My gift you are living
Praise faith and align
Harmonize hearts
Oppression resigns
New rhythm of love
Your halo now shines

Surrender

Soften your approach to life
Usher in what's overdue
Romance the thought of letting go
Resonate and feel renewed
Ease into a better place
Navigate your spirit true
Deliver up your higher self
Eternal living is what you do
Realign with the inner you

Synchronicity

Save yourself to find true being
Your thoughts and feelings here entwine
No more needed than you present
Communicate with the divine
Harmony and balance
Resonate with love and care
Open heart and open mind
Now you're woke and you're aware
Infinitely living
Coincidence erased
Insync with this world spinning
Take a moment to give grace
You're conscious here of time and space

There's a Finish Line

Take a mind trip through your history
Hopes and fears have brought you here
Each moment lived were lessons
Recall the times you've laughed through tears
Explore from here your choices
Stand firm to focus if unsure

Advance again when ready

Footsteps all lead to heaven's door
Invest in staying present
No second-guessing life defined
Instinct will guide your body
Spirit guides your soul and mind
Heaven's watching and applauding

Let love flow freely is the key
Its complexity is simple
Nothing but love will set you free
End your time alive with me

This is Eden

Terrestrial orb in orbit
Habitation for your soul
In dire need of presence
Stripping microns to find gold

Impoverishment of mankind
Suspension needed for repair

Eden raped of precious stardust
Digging further in despair
Endangered is existence
Now is time to show you care

This is how you do It

Take a leap of faith's the first step
Honesty you'll need as true
Incremental is your measure
Step by step till death you'll do

Incarnations here for karma
Souls are here for penance too

Hone in on being present
Observe the miracle of you
Wisdom is a worth worth gleaming

You can jump a life or two
Open up to being eternal
Use this life to be renewed

Destinations past the graveyard
On to heaven for review

Incidentally it's self-judgement
Take your next step with this news

Together

The right characters
One and one equals one
Genetically different
Evolve having fun
Taking two for creation
He and her girl or son
Eggs born all inside her
Ready set go and run

Unbelievable

Use your heart to hear his calling
Nourish your soul with his love
Bring out the best of you believing
Elevate within above
Level up to be delivered
In sync with spirit by your side
Enlightened and enlightening
Vested interest in your life
Almighty is his presence
Brilliance found within is key
Love for God unlocks the answers
Eternal knowledge sets you free

Victory

Vindication of self
Incredible views
Championing life
Transmitting truths
Oppression's recession
Rally of youth
Yes you win being you

Wipe the Sleep Away

Worlds away from the o'clock
Imagine history today
Put yourself into the present
End your time as self-enslaved

Take a breath to fuel you ready
Honor heaven you were made
Eternal soul you have awoken

Seek out seekers to seek gain
Leave the sleepers sleeping soundly
Early risers know this game
Expect to witness lost and lonely
Prepare yourself to feel their pain

Attend to nurture mother nature
Warm your soul close by her flame
Awaken to this big bad world
You're awake to make it good again

Wonder (i)

We find ourselves
On borrowed time
No need to look back
Don't fall behind
Every soul has a common goal
Receive good karma when aligned

Wonder (ii)

What's your infinite internal
Out in space is near the same
Neuroscience is our journal
Dreamers often thought insane
Ever wondered why you're living
Round and round you go again

Willing and Able

Wisdom gained to reach here
Intelligent account
Learnt by truly looking
Learnt to leave behind no doubt
Indifference needs arresting
Nothing less than care is out
God be for and not against us

Angels here and there about
Nominate yourself as willing
Do what's right for one and all

Audition for a starring role
Before the final call
Leave behind a better world
Eternal living reinstalled

You are Dying

Yes it's true you're dying
Only God knows the date
Understand this is living

Awaken awake
Round you go in the garden
Eden births and ends you bare

Do your very level best
You have moments to spare
Imagine now whilst you're living
Now is now's the time to care
Gain good karma if you share

The End… Is only the Beginning.

The Five New Commandments

11th Commandment is faith
Faith is needed to succeed

12th Commandment is fixed
Do not follow in mans greed

13th Commandment is for you to explore
Stay within boundaries or fall on your sword

14th Commandment is protection from treason
Seek only your purpose and not for lives reason

15th Commandment is the last for survival
Be in sync with your soul before judged on arrival

www.ingramcontent.com/pod-product-compliance
Lightning Source LLC
Chambersburg PA
CBHW060348080526
44583CB00012B/222